# *Sheer Cliffs and Shearwaters*

## A Skomer Island Journal

## Richard Kipling

with illustrations by Michael Roberts

Brambleby Books

ISBN 978-1-908241-21-4
eISBN 978-1-908241-29-0

First published in 2013 by BRAMBLEBY BOOKS
www.bramblebybooks.co.uk

Cover design and layout by Tanya Warren – Creatix
Cover photo by Richard Kipling
©Illustrations by Michael Roberts

Printed on FSC paper and bound by
Berforts Information Press, U.K.

# Dedication

For the Skomer team 2011

The Skomer Team 2011, from left to right: James Roden (long term volunteer) Chris Taylor (warden) Sarah Harris (assistant warden) Holly Kirk (researcher) Richard Kipling, Dave Boyle (researcher) Annette Fayet (researcher) Sue Williams (hostel warden).

# About the Author

I was born in Macclesfield, Cheshire, in 1977, the eldest of two children. Growing up in Macclesfield, between the contrasting landscapes of the Peak District and the dairy pastures of the Cheshire plain, and at the ill-defined border between 'The North' and the Midlands, has had a big impact on my outlook, and on my writing. In my work I am interested in seeking points of interaction between different states, subjects, ideas, landscapes and people; at these points there is diversity, openness and potential. Perhaps this tendency towards transition and diversity is also reflected in my education and

 career to date. I studied Economics and Politics at the University of York between 1996 and 1999, and after graduation found work as a clerical officer in the busy radiology department of Macclesfield hospital. Three years later I changed course, joining the National Trust in Shropshire as a long-term volunteer, where I learnt a range of practical conservation skills and developed a strong interest in ecology. A short spell coordinating training for a division of the Greater Manchester Police followed, but I soon felt compelled to return to the conservation sector. In 2003 I moved to Aberystwyth, gaining a degree in Countryside Conservation in 2006. With a number of summer ranger jobs at different nature reserves under my belt, I

took my interest in the environment a stage further, returning to Aberystwyth University to undertake a Ph.D. in Pollination Ecology. On completion of my studies I took up the seasonal post of field assistant on Skomer Island, taking time out to walk the Camino de Santiago in the autumn of 2011 and to pursue my interest in writing.

# Contents

Preface                                    11

April                                      13

May                                        36

June                                       82

July                                      122

August                                    153

References and Further Reading            167

Species List                              169

Acknowledgements                          175

Useful Organisations and Contacts         177

Annette's Recipes                         180

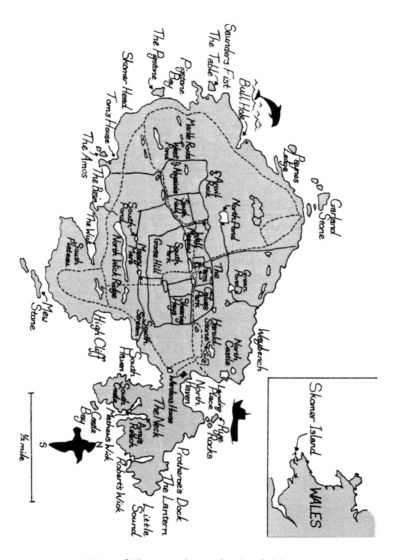

Map of Skomer, drawn by Sarah Harris

# *Preface*

I first visited the island of Skomer in the September of 2004, as part of a team undertaking a survey of the unique Skomer Vole. During that week of late summer sunshine I began to get a feel for what a special place Skomer is. It occupies a position that appears romantically distant even on the map, lying as it does off the southern tip of St Bride's Bay, isolated by the turbulent waters of Jack Sound in one of the most far-flung and beautiful parts of Wales. In 2011, an opportunity arose for me to return to the island as a field assistant with the Wildlife Trust of South and West Wales; I jumped at the chance. This book is an account of my time working on Skomer, of life in the small, transient community that occupies the island through the summer months, and of the natural events that mark the passage from spring to late summer in that part of the world.

Skomer Island is famed for its population of Atlantic Puffins, but there is far more to the island. It has been an Iron Age settlement, a medieval Rabbit warren, a farm and, latterly, an internationally important nature reserve. I hope the following pages will show some of the natural and historical diversity of Skomer, a diversity that continues to make the island a source of fascination for naturalists, historians, archaeologists and day-trippers alike. This diary is also a personal reflection, tracing my own journey through the seasons on this remote and beautiful rock. I hope it passes on a little of the magic of this hidden treasure of the Welsh coast.

# *April*

Atlantic Puffin

15<sup>th</sup>: It was a rushed end to life in Aberystwyth. Over the last few days there has been a gradual stripping away of ties, associations, possessions; the bulk of my kit is now under a massive tarpaulin in a garage, and I have said goodbye to my friends. With my Ph.D. completed, it is time to begin a new chapter of my life. Thursday was melancholy after the leaving party, even though I will be back to visit – I have known these people for a long time now, and leaving Aberystwyth is in some ways like leaving a family. I give up the past reluctantly and only accept the hand of change in retrospect.

It was a sunny day for a drive down the coast but, being late, I was frustrated by lorries and Sunday drivers out two days early. My spirits rose as I reached the Preselis, perhaps my favourite of the Welsh mountains. Traversing the spine of these ancient hills and dropping down into South Pembrokeshire seemed to move the past a little further behind me. After losing my way in the centre of Haverfordwest, I reached Martin's Haven with only ten minutes to spare before the boat was due to leave. There was a great deal of lifting and carrying; I deposited my bags and boxes on the quayside and took my car to West Hook farm, finally running back to the seafront, laptop in hand, with one return trip for my forgotten mobile phone!

The path to the boat is uneven and narrow, and despite the help of the visitor centre manager, Reese, I was hot and sweating when I finally clambered into the *Dale Princess*. Then, quickly, we were pulling out of the haven, and the silver-grey waters of Jack Sound were gliding past. Here there was a stronger breeze, cooler air and mist over the craggy back of Skomer, my new home. A tanker lay in St Bride's Bay, and I remembered that they waited in the sheltered waters before entering Milford Haven; these leviathans had been silent companions on my coastal walk years before, and their presence now was oddly reassuring.

The *Dale Princess* rendezvoused mid-channel with a fishing boat of similar size, and I sat in the cabin as two buckets of live crabs, huge, brown-red, lugubrious, were passed across. Soon afterwards we reached North Haven; hands reached down to take my kit, bag by bag, up the steep concrete steps that led upwards from the landing point. Chris, the warden, Sarah, the assistant warden and Sue, the visitor manager, as well as three volunteers – Bridget, Pris and Martin – were there to help unload.

The accommodation had changed since my last visit: where the rather ramshackle research base had nestled on the isthmus joining the main island to the Neck (an eastern outcrop), a new solar-powered building stands. It includes living quarters and lab space for researchers – at the moment Ben, Holly and Annette studying Shearwaters, Chris's accommodation and an office and library on the first floor. Sarah and I, the volunteers and overnight guests, stay at the old farm. This lies up a stony track, open on either side to rock-studded country. Outcrops like those on the Presellis occupy the skyline, punctuating the open plateau of the central part of the island.

The farmhouse itself is just a shell now, with a Perspex roof inside to allow visitors to picnic. As I approached I remembered Lockley's description of their visit in 1946, of how they made the farm habitable after years of neglect. He had written of their survey efforts in the language of a military operation, reflecting the influence of the war on their thoughts and style of thinking. It was a little sad to think of their heroic clear out, patch-up and occupation of the old place, while seeing it once again returned to ruin.

Entering the courtyard of the farm via a gateway in a low stone wall, the house lies on your right. Opposite it is a two-storey building containing the visitor centre and accommodation for overnight guests and researchers. A single-storey row of rooms faces you across the grass; it must have originally been a stable block. The right side of this building holds the volunteer rooms and kitchen, to the left a self-contained flat I will be sharing with Sarah. I looked around my new home; a modern kitchen with glass doors leading off the courtyard, the rest of the rooms lying off one side of a corridor, with the exception of the lounge at the far end of the narrow building. Without heating my own room is somewhat damp, but I have a heavy duvet, and in the silence of the island it is easy to sleep.

Sue made an evening meal for me, Sarah, Chris and the three volunteers who are about to leave the island: delicious soup and homemade pizza, accompanied by a couple of beers. Chris I knew already as a fellow graduate of the Rural Sciences Department at Aberystwyth University. He is tall, thin; a keen climber from the West Country and, as warden, a welcoming host. Sue, aside from being a great cook (which she sees as both a blessing and a curse when communal meals need preparing!) is a straightforward Welsh woman, with an interesting past, including many years living in the Netherlands as a painter/decorator. An entertaining companion, but someone to stay on the right side of! Sarah, the assistant warden and my new flatmate, is another graduate of Aberystwyth and an open, friendly girl; irrepressibly enthusiastic and a knowledgeable birder. This group, the volunteers and a couple of cans of beer made for a friendly and entertaining meal. It was a great introduction to island life and, as usual, my doubts at times of change were shown to be passing frailties of the mind; if I can enjoy the present without looking too far forward, or back, I feel that there are many new and exciting experiences awaiting me here.

16th: I slept well, relaxing after the stress of packing, leaving, goodbyes and the tying of countless loose ends. I had breakfast and headed down to North Haven to meet Chris for my induction as field assistant. For the next four months my role will be to monitor a range of seabirds, including Guillemots and Kittiwakes, and there is a lot for me to learn. The morning was cool and misty, Great Black-backed Gulls[1] glided low and

---

[1] Given their long names, Great Black-backed and Lesser Black-backed Gulls are often referred to as 'Greaters' and 'Lessers', respectively; I will use these simpler names in the following pages.

massive over the rocks, and the grey sea stretched away into the haze of St Bride's Bay.

At the centre I had a morning of reading various files on Health and Safety and general island information, and a more interesting afternoon locating my survey sites with Chris. He was keen to get out around the island, leaving the paperwork and phone calls behind for a couple of hours: the job of island warden has many aspects, from administration to repairing buildings, visitor management to plumbing – and this range of activities can mean that spending time out on the reserve is a rare luxury. In North Valley a Short-eared Owl, brown, gold and beige, flapped and swooped low over the ground as we walked towards the north coast. Here I was introduced to my hide overlooking the Guillemot-crowded ledges of Bull Hole. To the south-west of the island lies my viewing position amongst the Puffin burrows of the Wick; there are two additional sites at which I will observe Kittiwakes, one on a rocky platform opposite High Cliff and the other in a small inlet at South Stream – according to Chris a good spot for swimming.

Walking between the sites we saw a 'Greater' pulling at the body of a Shearwater with its heavy, bloodied beak, while Puffins looked on apparently unfazed, the crocodile-like promontory of the Wick cliff-face framing the scene. Back at North Haven a Shearwater had been found on the surface – rare during the day – and on inspection it was clear its eyes had been taken out during a fight; one of the researchers despatched it quickly, as it had no chance of survival. Death, of course, is as ubiquitous as the teeming life of the island.

I finished the day with a stroll around the coast, chatting to Ian, a BBC cameraman, who was on Skomer putting together footage for the forthcoming series of *Springwatch*. He was capturing the sunset from Skomer Head, and we watched as the sun spectacularly fell, lemon-yellow, into a quicksilver sea of surging currents, the glittering path of light reaching out to the headland where we stood. As I walked back to the farm I noted that the unfortunate cameraman had been thwarted; a grey and distant wall of cloud had risen over the horizon, denying him a shot of the sun slipping below the waves. Tomorrow I need to absorb the various survey techniques that I will be using to observe the seabirds and produce a plan of my work over the next four months.

17th: The sunny weather of yesterday evening returned this morning. Although it was gone nine when I set out, the mounds of grass, Sea Campion and Thrift were still glistening silver with dew, and despite the sun the chill of the night lingered across the island. I began the day at Bull Hole, sitting in front of the hide on damp swathes of short, Rabbit-grazed turf. With the luxury of unobserved solitude I tested the workings of the telescope and tripod given to me for my work, grateful for the chance to make a series of clumsy mistakes with only the Kittiwakes and Guillemots to see me.

Finally I settled to scanning the ledges of the colony and trying to get a feel for the behaviour of the Guillemots. I watched those standing close together preen each other, exchange glances, nod and appear to tap their beaks together. Sometimes one would hesitantly shuffle to the edge of a ledge and, with a tilted head and a series of false starts, eventually jump and flutter to another white-stained perch. Over the morning the number of birds at the site decreased; at one point a 'Greater' glided purposefully up to the ledges, causing a flurry of panicked movement and calling. I moved into the hide, feeling a chill breeze off the sea. A mist threatened and a foghorn sounded across the bay, but the weather did not worsen on the island. In my shelter I read some of the notes on survey methods before picking my way back up the researchers' path to the plateau.

View from the hide at Bull Hole

Returning to the farm, I saw two small yellow-green tinged birds close to the ruined outbuildings – Sarah tells me they were probably Willow Warblers – while from the undergrowth in North Valley came the trilling call of a Grasshopper Warbler. After lunch I spent some time at the Wick, warm and sheltered in comparison to the northern coast, and on my way round to Skomer Head discovered Three-lobed Water-crowfoot in Wick Stream, albeit a poor specimen, bedraggled and strangled by algae.

Each evening on the island there is a 'Bird Log', a chance to catch up with the various inhabitants of the island and to hear which birds have been seen during the day[2]. I headed down to North Haven with Sarah for my first experience of this island ritual, meeting Mick, a vole surveyor whom I had first encountered five years ago, during my week as a volunteer on the Skomer Vole survey. It was good to see him again, a reminder of what had been an enjoyable and sociable week. I also met Jess, who will be training Chris and me on the more intensive Guillemot survey method we will be using at Bull Hole. From Sheffield University, she is surveying Guillemots at the Amos for Tim Birkhead, an authority on these birds. She is slim, with long dark hair and a quick sense of humour, and she soon made the task of Guillemot monitoring seem much less daunting than it had been. Ben (one of the Shearwater researchers) was discussing new data showing that the theory of magnetic navigation in pigeons was probably incorrect. Apparently molecules with magnetic properties are not connected to the bird's neurons and so cannot relay directional information. Instead they act as macrophages (large cells that consume other cells and material) found throughout the body of each bird. How they navigate remains a mystery.

With Bird Log completed, I walked back to the farm with Sarah and Jess. The moon was full and golden over the sea south of Skokholm, which lay low and serene amidst the waves, its lighthouse flashing red and bright at its westerly tip. Behind it the light at St Ann's head replied from the mainland, and over the back of Skomer to the north the South Bishop light

---

[2] 'Bird Log' is an island tradition, at which the warden reads through a list of birds, and people shout out which they have seen. As well as providing long-term records of bird sightings on the island, it is also a bit of a social event.

completed the regular comforting pattern across the dark sea, marking each point of silent land.

18th: It was a quiet day on the island today; on Mondays there are no boats, so the only visitors are those that land from private yachts and those who have stayed overnight. In the morning I walked out towards the Garland Stone, stopping where the path reaches a low wall and crosses North Stream. This is a good spot for birdwatching, with several low, bushy Goat Willow trees. I watched the Willow Warblers, Whitethroats and other small birds for a while to get used to the behaviour of each, before continuing to the coast. The sky was clear blue, but there was a cold breeze, and I only paused momentarily on the cliffs; five or six Gannets were fishing out beyond the Garland Stone, and further west, towards Payne's Rock there were two Harbour Porpoises swimming in the turbulent waters of the tidal race. I paused again at Bull Hole, but there were no Guillemots on the ledges, and I returned to the farm for lunch.

The afternoon passed in leisurely fashion. Chris came over and we discussed the new Guillemot survey with Jess. In fact it is not much different to the Wildlife Trust method, except that I need to visit Bull Hole every day and observe each bird until I am sure whether it has an egg or not – that will be the time consuming part! We chatted, and the afternoon drifted by in the sunshine. Where we sat by the courtyard wall there was no breeze, and visitors stopped to pass on their bird sightings. Ian, the BBC cameraman, and Dave Boyle joined us for tea and biscuits provided by Jess. Dave has been coming to Skomer for eight years to carry out monitoring work, spending his winters in the warmer climes of New Zealand. He looks well adapted to island life: short and wiry, with faded clothes and a permanent tan. His time on the island makes him a trusted source of information about pretty much all of its flora and fauna, and he is an experienced birder. Later, I walked out to Skomer Head and the Wick, although I found no Puffins for the 'classic' Skomer snap!

Bird Log at nine was followed by a couple of drinks at North Haven, the evening being rounded off by a walk back to the farm under a nearly full moon. The hummocky ground of the old fields close to the track showed an amazing pattern of rounded, folded shapes in the pale moonlight, and in St Bride's Bay the tankers lay awash with light on the dark water; a good end to the day.

19th: It was another sunny day on the island, and the Guillemots have come back in, re-populating their ledges at the Wick and Bull Hole. I spent an hour or so observing them at Wick Corner, and a further hour watching the ledges at Wick 1 and 2G. At Bull Hole I interspersed further observations with reading, particularly going through a scientific paper on Guillemots written by Tim Birkhead in the 1970s. The paper looked at the breeding success of birds in different types of location. It concluded that there was an increased risk of predation where there were few birds on a ledge, providing a barrier to colonising new areas of cliff-face. This could explain the growth and increasing density of existing breeding sites. Tim is visiting the island in a few weeks, so I need to know my Guillemots by then!

Around the island the vegetation is springing up; I saw Early Forget-me-not, Thrift and Common Scurvygrass in flower, in addition to Bluebells, Lesser Celandine and Red Campion. There was a Small Copper butterfly at the Wick, and after lunch I found two Common Carder Bee workers foraging on the Common Gorse bushes in South Park field. 'Carder' bees are so called because they roof their nests with moss.

South Stream Cliff

In the afternoon I headed down to South Stream, cutting along the research path towards the sea. Close to the stream, Hemlock Water Dropwort and Purple Loosestrife were starting to appear. I discovered a large, mottled brown egg, tinged green-beige, which Dave later said was probably that of a 'Lesser'. Closer to the sea, where the valley narrows into a gully, I saw a Whitethroat singing from the Brambles and several Willow Warblers. By the shore I met Sarah and we sat and watched the Puffins in the bay. Some, swimming with their mates, were showing off their brightly coloured bills, dipping them into the water so that the surface shone and the colours were exaggerated. Sarah pointed out how they landed, slowing their whirring flight, splaying their feet and then hitting the water and dunking face first under the waves, their momentum spoiling the effect of their finessed approach. The spot is perhaps my favourite on the island so far, sheltered and peaceful, with a view over the clear water to Skokholm, and to the Neck and the mainland to the south-east. South Stream tumbles over the rocks to the sea, and here even the cries of the Oystercatchers and the frantic whirring flights of the auks only seem to add to the tranquillity.

As afternoon turned to early evening, we walked up to Moory Mere hide, where Sarah showed me a crow's nest built from various bones and other debris, hidden in one of the Willows. There was a Shoveler on the mere – these are smartly coloured ducks with large, wide bills that they use to dig in the mud for food, giving them their name – and two Blackcaps in the scrub close to the hide. After tea – and a short diversion to photograph Puffins at the Wick – it was time for Bird Log and afterwards a couple of whiskies down at North Haven. Walking back to the farm the Manxie[3] cries were all around, the bay lit up by the floodlit tankers.

20th: A day off, and I took the nine o'clock boat to Martin's Haven, chatting to a GP and his wife who had been staying on the island for a couple of nights. We talked about the approaching NHS reforms, reminding me oddly of my coastal walk around St Bride's Bay ten years previously, a holiday taken just after I had finished work at Macclesfield Hospital. Back on the mainland I enjoyed the drive to Haverfordwest, noting how, only a few miles from the island, spring was more advanced and the vegetation more luxuriant, with Alexanders and Garlic Mustard mixed with Red Campion in the greening hedgerows.

---

[3] A familiar term for the Manx Shearwater.

24

Haverfordwest is centred round a steeply sloping river valley into which the main street drops headlong, the parish church watching over its descent. Away from the pedestrianised shopping area and riverside cafes, where I enjoyed a fry-up, despite the warm weather, lies a maze of narrow streets. These are lined with an assortment of white-washed and terraced cottages, small churches with rural graveyards of freshly mown grass, grey stone walls hot and dry in the sun, little passageways and winding steps.

I spent an enjoyable few hours exploring the town before it was time to return to the island, laden with food gathered during the obligatory hour in the supermarket, to 'enjoy' the first swim of the year, edging into the ice-cold waters of North Haven with Jess and one of the volunteers who dived in from up on the rocks with a courage I didn't quite possess! After Bird Log, I spent a while watching the night sky with Sarah and Nia, another of the weekly volunteers; Mars was bright, The Plough and Cassiopea massive and distant above us, satellites gliding silently, catching the light of the sun from their lofty orbit, the brief, bright, shard of a shooting star, and the Shearwaters crying out all around in the darkness.

21$^{st}$: Sunny again, and hot, as I walked across the island, finding Scarlet Pimpernel in flower near Wick Stream. This was the scenic route to Bull Hole, where I wanted to make an early draft of the Guillemot colony map. The method of surveying is to mark the territory of each pair of Guillemots on a photo of the plot (they defend an area of only 50cm$^2$, and are therefore tightly packed in when both adults are present). These marked sites, called 'Apparently Occupied Territories' or AOTs, are numbered and checked on each visit for eggs and, eventually, chicks. Early in the season the birds still move around the ledges a little; with mates coming and going and other birds 'loafing' at the margins of breeding areas, it can be extremely hard at first to correctly define each AOT. There was no sign as yet of any eggs being laid, although Jess and Dave have seen three at the Amos.

On the way back to the farm I saw two male Reed Buntings in the willow scrub near North Stream, smart with black heads and chestnut backs, flitting from branch to branch along with a couple of Whitethroats and Willow Warblers. The evening brought another freezing swim, and spaghetti bolognese cooked by Sarah before Bird Log. Tomorrow may be a busy day if the Guillemots have started to lay.

22nd: I carried out a full round of survey plots, marking up the photos of each with AOTs. There were no eggs at any of my sites, but it was good to get used to watching the birds and marking up the photos. I think at Wick Corner and 2G the recording task is going to be difficult: the plots are further away from the observation point than at Bull Hole, there are many densely packed areas and it is awkward working on the open hillside in comparison to the relative comfort of Bull Hole hide. Returning from that hide I was met by a swathe of dusky purple-blue; Bluebells stretching like a sea inland from the Garland Stone, lapping the rocky outcrops and punctuated by the white heads of 'Lessers', the colour of the flowers vivid under grey skies and drizzling rain.

Back at the farm everyone was preparing for a BBQ out in the yard, and I took half an hour to practice my Spanish – I intended to walk across Spain in the autumn, following the way of St James to Santiago de Compostela. Despite a few light showers, the BBQ was enjoyable, and I met Holly, the third of the Oxford researchers studying the Manx Shearwaters. She is tall, with short red hair and an infectiously outgoing personality, always ready with a quick reply to any friendly teasing. We all ended up in the old wardens' hut, drinking wine and telling ghost stories by candlelight. It reminded me of the warden's lodge at Barnswood scout camp, where as Venture Scouts we used to drink Schnapps and talk late into the night – days when life seemed simple and the experiences and thoughts of the last fifteen years still awaited me. I enjoyed the company of the group and the light, easy conversation of the evening in flickering candlelight with the ever-present wailing of the Manxies filling every moment of quiet.

23$^{rd}$: I got up fairly late after the festivities of the previous night, whilst Sarah, somewhat hung-over, headed off to do boats[4]; she is one of those people who is always exuberant and enthusiastic, and after a few drinks those qualities become exaggerated. It is good to spend time with someone who always finds the best in things and to whom everything is a new source of excitement – a tonic to my own outlook, sometimes tinged with negativity. Again there were no eggs at my Guillemot sites, and indeed there were few birds at Wick Corner – for the first few weeks of the season the birds come and go from the ledges, gradually becoming more settled as they begin to lay eggs. I will treat my early maps of AOTs as a practice and wait to record fully when the birds finally settle.

Sitting at the Wick, I got a great view of Choughs foraging amongst the rocks and short grass of the cliff-tops; these are spectacular corvids, night black with long, curved red beaks, red

---

[4] One of the daily island tasks involving taking the luggage of overnight guests to and from the landing steps, manning the sales point and giving introductory talks to the day visitors, up to 250 of whom are ferried over on the *Dale Princess* each day.

legs and a distinctive 'chee-ow' call as they fly and tumble acrobatically through the air. The Rabbit-grazed turf of the island coast is ideal habitat for them to hunt for worms and insects just under the surface of the earth. At Moory Mere hide I saw a pair of Shovelers mating, and a Curlew enjoying an extensive wash and preen in the shallows of the pool. In the willow scrub I spotted Whitethroats, Chiffchaffs (like Willow Warblers but browner, with constantly flicking tails) and the usual fluttering warblers. Walking back to the farm, the Bluebells on Gorse Hill were now matched in striking colour by the pink of Red Campion, scattered amongst the blue where the path crosses the tumble-down field boundary.

24th: Easter day, with clear skies and a blustery northerly wind. I sent messages to friends and family on the way to the Wick; it seems odd and a little sad not to be at home for Easter and not to be going to church. But the newly blooming flowers tell the story of the resurrection themselves, and as if in celebration I found my first two Guillemot eggs at Bull Hole. Jess found a third, and each of the three was different; the first white, the one Jess found turquoise blue and the third a paler sky blue, all mottled with brown speckles and streaks. Two of the eggs were on ledges one above the other, close on the cliff, and I wondered if some hormonal signal triggered laying, which the literature says is more synchronised in large, dense colonies than in small ones. I had an interesting chat with Jess about the Guillemots and survey methods, and it was nice to share the egg discovery… and crisps!

Walking back to the farm, the air was crystal clear. Every detail of the landscape around St Bride's Bay was picked out; Ramsey and the Bishops and Clerks islands at the tip of St David's peninsular, Grassholm, and the unmistakeable outline of the Preselis. In the deep blue bay tankers were vivid red, blue, white and black, rather than ill-defined grey forms in the mist. I returned to the farm glad to have some eggs recorded and my territories mapped.

25th: The northerly wind meant no boats today, and we had the island to ourselves. Again there were no eggs at any of my Wick sites, but at Bull Hole I found a fourth egg, high up in the section and quite close to the egg Jess found yesterday outside the survey area.

Walking back from the hide, I reflected on island life. For once I was relatively free of concerns; something about the separateness of the island community allowed me to deal with each day on its own merits. My usual imaginings about the future were minimised; I was able to appreciate things as they were. Part of this was the nature of my work. Concentrating on the movements of the Guillemots, observing things in their world of instinct and routine meant that the 'now' filled my thoughts. These birds did not consider the future but reacted to events. They survived, bred, lived and died without apprehension or a questioning of their place in the world. Their mistakes were natural, not distorted by conscious thought. It was a soothing world to observe, although of course I am concerned with producing good quality data, and only hard work will get me to that goal.

The island provides the mental space to take your time and observe things that are usually ignored. Between Skomer Head and Bull Hole I stopped and knelt by the path, watching the miniature landscape of Rabbit-grazed turf and tiny flowers. Pink, fleshy nodes of English Stonecrop were like the huge cacti of a North American desert, and ants clambered over the mountain ranges of tiny rocks. Rabbit droppings were surreal spherical sculptures on the savannahs of centimetres of grass, and the tiny flowers of Knotted Pearlwort were massive starbursts of white, thrusting from forests of dark green foliage. And at this scale was time also different? Were the foraging ants, away from their nests for periods of minutes, experiencing lengthy treks, explorations of hours? Perhaps this was the explanation for my ability, here, to consider each day alone as an experience in itself and not as a prerequisite for reaching some future goal. Perhaps the smaller scale of island life brought each experience and event outwards, to surround me, so that despite my human perception I was able to 'zoom in' to find more in each moment. A well-worn idea of course, but to experience it is a rare opportunity in the modern, connected world. I hope I can sustain the new perspective, that I can find that simple enjoyment, rather than being dragged into cycles of anticipation that stifle the present with fears for the future and regrets of the past.

26th: Much of Tuesday was spent at Bull Hole and the Wick. In the afternoon I went down to the library at North Haven; I have started looking at survey data from previous years, as there appears to be some confusion in the comparison of the Wildlife Trust's (WT) data and those from the Amos. The WT data include 'Regular' sites in the calculation of breeding success, where birds are present but not observed with eggs or chicks; these sites are not included in the Amos survey calculations. The library is a sociable place to work; Holly and Annette were there processing data, and Chris and Sarah came in after the last boat had gone.

In the evening I went out to look for the Little Owl towards Abyssinia, an intriguingly named field west of the farm. I was unsuccessful, but while I was enjoying the beautiful sunset, with North Valley a wide gentle sweep of Bluebells and Red Campion all around me, I turned to see the Short-eared Owl on the gable-end of the ruined buildings close to the farm.

After Bird Log and before turning in for the night, we heard a strange call near the farm, a whirring, screeching sound, apparently attracted by the mechanical noise of a wind-up torch! Our best guess was that it was a Barn Owl, cruising under the stars of the clear moonless night.

27th: A day off, and I slept until ten, then spent some time working on the Guillemot data before wandering out into a warm, clear-skied morning. I strolled out towards Moory Mere, noting bees, plants and birds; I have had the idea of compiling a list of all the plants I can find, to compare with the list of flora in Lockley and Buxton's book from the 1950s. It will be interesting to look at how things have changed in the sixty or so years since their survey of the island. After lunch I went down to the Amos with Jess to see the site and the hide. The survey path winds around the outcrop that overlooks the Amos and then drops steeply until, after a final turn, the fragile-looking hide is revealed, set against an overhanging block of grey rock and steadied by wire lines, with a worn wooden bench in front. The rocks tumble down to the sea, which to the north and south cuts inwards so that you look out from a high, narrow headland over turquoise water, where Puffins and Guillemots dive and swim.

The Amos itself is a spit of rock that juts out to the north of the hide, before stretching back round to the south to capture a narrow bay within the bend of its arm. It is topped by a lopsided natural arch standing close to the highest point of the promontory. This is a mount of bare rock connected to the Skomer mainland by a narrow bridge of basalt, eroded below to form another larger arch. And on this rocky mount gather the Guillemots, lining the ledges and scree slopes, facing inwards, looking up towards the higher arch like the crowds in a biblical scene, gathered in awe at some heavenly portent; I half expected, glancing up, to see some shining figure, preaching to the sharp-billed brown and white congregation below. Beyond this scene the sea sparkled in the afternoon sun, and over the shoulder of Grassholm the dark silhouette of the Smalls Lighthouse was just visible in the haze.

Two previous Guillemot researchers, after months of fieldwork in the hide, had written a series of rhymes on its plywood walls and ceiling: strange poems scrawled over walls painted to show a view as if from an egg being incubated, on one wall a mural of a bird's leg with the ring number '666'. Humorous but slightly sinister, or at least surreal, especially with the decaying paraphernalia of earlier surveys dotting the surrounding cliffs; a cross of wooden beams, a concrete platform, discarded metal poles. After a season of surveying, one of the researchers had left science, the other became a Buddhist. And certainly the hours of surveying encourage a meditative detachment, the scenery an escape from reality, from concepts of time beyond the cycles of days and seasons. I slept for a while on a bed of Sea Campion, with the sound of the sea and the birds all around, an idea for a short story half forming in my mind. The day ended with a sighting of the Barn Owl, swooping silently from the owl box in the slate-tiled gable-end of the old farm.

28th and 29th:  The end of the week passed quickly, with more Guillemot eggs laid each day. On Friday, Jess, Chris and I braved the waters of North Haven again. This time, though it was still fairly cold, I stayed in for a while longer and felt I had

had a proper swim. Bird Log on Thursday was rounded off by a hunt around North Haven to track down the source of another strange birdcall heard by one of the volunteers. Unsurprisingly we returned none the wiser, eight people with torches wandering in the dark, enough to cause any self-respecting bird to take cover; Most likely it had been the Barn Owl from the farm hunting over the darkened slopes above the bay.

30th: No boats today due to more strong northerly winds, and Chris joined me for the Guillemot observations. It was good to have company and a second pair of eyes to spot the elusive eggs. Although large – one sixth the size of an adult bird – and ranging in colour from lurid turquoise or mint blue to white, the eggs are easily concealed under the thick downy feathers of the parent. And spotting them is all the more challenging when the birds are packed together on a wide ledge, five or six birds deep. They form an undulating surface of dark brown heads, the white flashes on the birds' wings punctuating this charcoal sea and the constant movement of long sharp beaks engaged in delicate mutual grooming, or not so delicate territorial defence.

Fights can be vicious and prolonged; Jess has seen protagonists covered with blood. Often the first cuts are at the base of the bill, as the birds lock them together to wrestle, standing on other birds, knocking eggs off ledges in some cases and oblivious to anything but the defeat of their opponent. The contrast with the apparent care with which mates and other birds that share the same ledge groom each other, is striking; trusting the other bird to search and delve through their smooth dark feathers even close to the eyes. Both care and aggression are easy to anthropomorphise, and in truth much of a bird's behaviour may be unthinking reflex; often birds appear to act as if their egg is still present when it has been lost, or return to gentle preening seconds after the most vicious looking of fights.

# The Guillemot

*Nestled in the frame of rocks*
*Geometry of crevice, angled ledge*
*Javelin beaks black lines*
*That cross the fissures, linking bird*
*With stone and jagged edge*
*Lifeless world of sea and sky*
*That holds no malice or regret*
*No grudge or mercy, helping hand*
*Alone, and with this blackened*
*Point of keratin they share*
*Their love and share their hate*
*And shield their egg with little*
*Help from clumsy feet.*
*Preening with a deadly barb the*
*Smooth and dusty chocolate*
*Feathers of their mates and fellows*
*On the ledge; delicate*
*Caresses close to shining eyes*
*With needle points that stab*
*At gulls and capture silver Sprats*
*From deep beneath the turquoise*
*Sea; strange implement to find*
*Adorning rounded beings*
*Of curved divide of white*
*And brown, wing and breast*
*All softness, warmth and comfort*
*That which meets the outside world*
*That tames those empty forces and*
*In merciless pursuit can match*
*The mindless crashing waves*
*Is that which in defence*
*Will nurture what is new.*

# *May*

Bluebells

1<sup>st</sup>: Sunday, and again there were more eggs at Wick Corner and Bull Hole. Around lunchtime I met Sarah and Chris, perched on the rocky outcrop near the path to my hide. They were surveying the colony of 'Lessers' on the opposite side of the gully that widens out to Bull Hole cliffs. The gulls nest on the ground, dotted amongst the Bluebells and Red Campion, their seaside-white heads and bright beaks contrasting with the green, pink and blue of vegetation. They do not appear to be concerned by the bamboo canes that mark out a grid across the colony, allowing the surveyor, situated at some high vantage point, to map nest sites in relation to these markers. Nests and their contents are recorded to be checked again for large chicks later in the season.

In the evening we held a party for Jess's birthday. Everyone cooked some food (I made potatoes with spinach, garlic, onions, butter and garam masala mixed spice; there was an Indian theme), and we sat at a long trestle table under the Perspex roof, erected inside the ruined farm to provide day visitors with a sheltered picnic spot. It was nice to enjoy the old building, and I felt close to Lockley and the other survey pioneers of 1946. As a somewhat unusual birthday present we had painted a model Guillemot, made earlier in the year out of papier-mâché and chicken wire, and even added a colour ring (yellow 274, a bridled Guillemot I had spotted at Bull Hole); part of Jess's job is to record the position of as many previously ringed individuals as she can. A green-painted, hard-boiled egg was added to complete the odd ensemble! We were joined in our celebration by the volunteers who made a large, sausage-based cottage pie and, encouraged by beer and red wine, there was a friendly and entertaining atmosphere. As is becoming a tradition, we finished the night by flickering candlelight in the old wardens' hut; a lovely evening.

2nd: I awoke fairly late (predictably after the celebrations of last night!) to the sound of a strong wind blustering around the farm buildings. It was a cold morning at the Wick and frustrating, as the wind prevented me from getting a steady view of the Guillemots, knocking the telescope askew countless times, often at the crucial moment when a bird momentarily shifted to allow a view of any potential egg. The afternoon, in the shelter of Bull Hole hide, was much better; now that more birds have eggs the task takes longer (I have to confirm each egg is still there), but slowly my sample size is increasing – 47 eggs seen in total. Apart from some confusion with the positions of some of the AOTs on the wider ledges, I have quite a clear idea of the colony and nest sites.

$3^{rd}$: The winds were strong again today, and, despite securing my survey maps with elastic bands, three of them were whipped out of the file down at the Wick. A Benny Hill-type scene quickly developed with me sprinting over the uneven ground chasing the photos, while avoiding burrows and hoping the vital bits of paper would not blow into the sea. As luck would have it, they finally fluttered down into a crevice on the cliff-top, and I collected them up with much relief. The thought of remarking all the AOTs on each map was unwelcome to say the least, and I abandoned the site and headed to the shelter of Bull Hole. It turned out to be a long day; I decided to 'nail' the site and stayed for seven long hours. For the first time I allowed myself to become stressed by the task, and the evening was a fairly negative one despite the promise of a day off tomorrow.

$4^{th}$: I caught the morning boat which ploughed through a heavy swell in a brisk wind to take me into Martin's Haven and the welcome solidity of the mainland. I still felt a little on edge and got around the supermarket as quickly as possible before driving to the car park behind the sweeping, modern leisure centre in Haverfordwest. My inward-looking mental state was worked off by a brisk walk around the town and in the light interactions with shop staff experienced by the solitary browser. I enjoyed immensely the fresh greens of the Lime and Horse-chestnut trees that spread over the cut-through into the centre. To one side this path bordered the graveyard of a small church, and from here the trees generously stretched their soft, verdant cloaks of leaves. On the other were the grey stone walls and brimming vegetation of townhouse back gardens.

I strolled contentedly, exchanging smiles with a shop worker who was sitting on a low wall to enjoy a mid-morning smoke. The path headed gently towards the spreading vista of the town in its wide valley, perhaps only 50 yards in all, but bringing a comfortable peace within those few short paces. I love these hidden complexities that hide behind the street-facing façade of an old town; the details of wrought iron railings, narrow winding streets, stone steps and buildings shaped to fit around hill and road.

Nearly at the main street I found an Oxfam bookshop. Comforted by the jumbled shelves of worn books I picked out three: Conrad's *The Secret Agent*, Wilkie Collins' *The Moonstone* and Tolstoy's *Anna Karenina*. Leaving somewhat reluctantly, I undertook my errands for the day and, still feeling a little unsettled, spent a few minutes in the parish church, although the peace offered was tempered by the shouts and crashing of builders working on the roof! The afternoon brought me the new perspective I was looking for. As I headed left and up from the main street towards the leisure centre I passed a small music shop and on impulse went in. The collection was mainly jazz, but there was also an extensive range of world music and an interesting selection of more general rock. I found a John Martyn CD, *Solid Air*, and a compilation of Cuban music, attracted to the latter by the colourful artwork: a scene of a Havana street with a bustling café, girls and 1930s cars, in smooth, stylized colour, bringing to me the nostalgic atmosphere of the pre-revolutionary music scene in Cuba. My haul was rounded off by the addition of a Ravi Shankar CD, which I thought might be good for relaxation during the long hours in the hide. While browsing I overheard the shop owner recommend to a couple that they eat at The Georges next door. We had a friendly conversation, about jazz and the world in general, that made me feel even more at home in this interesting west Wales town, and afterwards I took his advice on lunch.

On the outside The Georges is an ordinary pub set into the terrace, but I walked through the door (complete with a sign encouraging me to 'leave all emotional baggage here') into a mixture of new-age emporium, niche café and pub. Tables were randomly set into alcoves with sofas, stools and chairs mixed together, the lighting was soft and there was a lively hum of conversation in the low-ceilinged room. I ordered my lunch and wound my way down a small passageway and through rooms full of colourful clothes, aromatherapy oils and scented candles, to emerge into a quiet beer garden with a trickling fountain that added to the sense of tranquillity. The food was good, and I passed an hour or so eating and beginning *The Moonstone*. By the time I left to make my way back to the car I was relaxed and happy; the book, the kindness of the music shop owner and pub staff and the gentle atmosphere of Haverfordwest had given me a contented and positive perspective; on the island, on my work and on my future, as opportunities to be enjoyed, free of the stress of wanting more.

Before I returned to Martin's Haven I took a detour to Little Haven, a small coastal village at the mouth of a narrow valley, where the road twists and turns down to the sea past a crowd of white-washed houses. On the front, a pub faces out over the beach; the last time I had visited the village was on September 12th, 2001, and my journal of that coastal walk mentions the US flag that flew at half-mast outside the pub that day. No dark shadow spoilt this afternoon, and I sheltered from the stiff breeze amongst the rocks on the beach, reading and appreciating the sun and the smooth strip of sand with the glittering sea at its edge. I returned to Martin's Haven only to find that the last boat had left early; luckily Carl agreed to do an extra run for me, and after a cup of tea at Lockley Lodge I was ferried back to the island.

5$^{th}$: As the morning was wet and windy, I began surveying at Bull Hole and, with relatively few birds on the cliffs, made good progress finding more eggs. John Martyn and my selection of Cuban music on my MP3 player helped me to focus on observation without my mind wandering, and it was an interesting contrast to watch the Guillemots sheltering from the

Puffins at the Wick

rain and wind to a soundtrack of lively Latino music. With the wind still fairly strong, surveying at Wick Corner in the afternoon was cold but successful, with a total of 24 eggs seen at the site by the time my observations were complete. As I scanned the cliff, the Puffins fluttered in from the sea, so that when I looked up I was surrounded amongst the Sea Campion and soft, cropped grass by a crowd of inquisitive white faces, seemingly unperturbed by my presence in the heart of their colony.

Heading home, Sarah's boyfriend, Gavin, cooked us all spaghetti bolognese; I was grateful for the chance to work on my comparison of Guillemot data from the Wildlife Trust and Sheffield methods. I slept well, free of the tension that had marred Tuesday evening, and feeling that I had found a healthier balance of work, and learnt the lesson that I can get good results without pushing too far. The evening ended with an enjoyable glass or two of wine with Sue and Jess and a long chat that ranged from Guillemots to life after Skomer.

6th: The weather was fine enough to survey the Wick, the wind from the south being cut off by the cliffs, but in the afternoon the same southerly wind whipped down the narrow valley of Bull Hole and shook the hide as I worked, glad of the new addition of music. I spent most of the evening writing up my report on the Guillemot data until seven when we all crowded into the old wardens' hut for a meal prepared by the volunteers. We ate well; spaghetti bolognese – again! – and bread and butter pudding, and after a couple of drinks began to talk of a Skomer Folk Festival, which in the crowded haze of late evening seemed the simplest idea in the world to put together. The end of another week, my third on the island, and much to do in the next!

$7^{th}$: Saturday morning, under grey scudding clouds and squalls of rain, was spent completing the Guillemot report for Tim Birkhead's arrival. That task finished, I headed for my afternoon stint at Bull Hole. A Golden Oriole was spotted in North Valley later in the day, and I joined Jerry, the Skokholm warden, separated from his island by the weather, and Chris to see if we could see it. First we wandered up to the hide at North Pond and watched Canada Geese plying the water with their almost luminous yellow-green chicks in tow, while gulls drifted overhead under a darkening sky. Thunder rumbled, and to the west the peach sky was capped by dark racing clouds and smears of distant rain. We walked down the North Stream research path, my first exploration of this route. The Bluebells and Red Campion are ubiquitous now, a pastel sheen of colour smudging the open landscape with blue and pink, and amongst them the first fresh green fronds of Bracken that will in time come to dominate. The others set the pace, and once again the alertness and sharp eyes of experienced birders struck me; they spotted and identified glimpses of movement and shape that I would never have noticed alone.

As the valley turns towards the coast, the stream has been dammed to create a small pool; below this volunteer-built tumble of stones, Goat Willow, Elder and Blackthorn fill the narrowing valley, creating a closer and more three-dimensional landscape than the open vistas of the rest of the island. I strolled along, taking in the greenery and the changing sky. Prehistory was close at hand, the mark of ancient settlers in the solid stone remains of an Iron Age storehouse. We crossed the stream and the path lay along a low wall, passing through a colony of 'Lessers'. Their heads protruded from the vegetation, some standing on the wall on their strikingly bright yellow legs, all climbing in a crescendo of noise to swoop and turn above us as we walked among nests, each filled with as many as three olive and brown mottled eggs. No Oriole, but an interesting part of the island explored.

8th: Somewhat conscious of the fact that Tim Birkhead is on the island, I was down at Bull Hole by eight. In the continuing high winds the sea was spectacular; waves laced with white and turquoise in the morning sun smashed into the dark rocks at the foot of the cliffs. After lunch I surveyed Wick Corner and, despite the partial shelter from the southerly wind provided by the Wick itself, my task was awkward and time consuming as I battled to keep hold of my papers, and to keep the telescope still.

At half past three we met to discuss the Guillemot data; luckily Tim was pleased with my analysis, and we agreed on the main points. Importantly I was given a set time (no more than four hours per day) to survey Bull Hole, with some leeway to class birds as 'incubating' if this was clear without an egg being seen. The meeting over I set out to find 'Greater' nests, with Chris agreeing to search the southern side of the island, while I concentrated on the north. On the way up from North Haven, I paused to visit the Harold Stone, an ancient stone of unknown use that stands out on the skyline as you approach the island by boat. It will be interesting on a clear day to see how it is positioned relative to the setting and rising sun and to the Preselis with their widespread traces of prehistoric settlement.

I continued towards the farm and then struck off along the research path to the left where the track passes through a low wall at the crest of the hill. My first attempts at nest location were relatively fruitless, with only one found on the ridge between Dave's small research hide and the path to Moory Mere; I had approached them with the setting sun behind the birds, and there were large numbers of 'Lessers' nesting close by, so that it quickly became impossible to work out where the 'Greaters' had been sitting when they all took to the sky. Having learnt my lesson, I stayed on the path to Skomer Head until I could look at target outcrops with the glare of the sun behind me. In this part of the island the 'Lessers' are also a little further away from the 'Greaters'. I found it was important to locate the sitting bird of the pair, as the other bird would stand some distance from the nest in an exposed position, flying up to distract my attention as I approached. Meanwhile the bird on the nest would quietly fly away in a different direction.

'Greater' nests are usually among the boulders and rocky surfaces of the ridges that dot the island, neat bowls of dried grass in which the eggs are placed. There are up to three eggs, larger than those of the 'Lessers' but with the same olive and brown mottled colouration. For some distance around each nest the ground was littered with the recent remains of Shearwaters and the older bleached bones of these birds, Rabbits and other species, so that it felt like I was approaching the lairs of dragons amongst the crags on the lonely plateau. The search was satisfying and rewarding, and it was good to walk and pursue, rather than sitting and waiting, which goes against my nature.

9th: I slept poorly last night as a result of the nocturnal activities of the Shearwaters; at this time of year the females are returning to their burrows to lay eggs, after two weeks away. During this time their movements are not well known; it is thought that they may seek different prey species to gain the nutrients they need to grow their egg, but where they travel to is unclear. In the past it was believed that they moved down to the Bay of Biscay, but this may not be true; the tracking work being undertaken by Holly, Ben and Annette should help shed light on their travels. GPS trackers are attached to the birds from which their movements can be downloaded when they return to their burrows. A saltwater sensor is also attached, so that the researchers can see how much time the birds spend in the water during their journeys.

The male Shearwaters await their mates in the burrow; when each female returns to lay her egg, both birds will share the task of incubation, taking turns of four to six days on the egg until it hatches. The upshot is that many birds return to the island each night, and a good proportion appear to crash into and scrabble about on the roof of our flat. Although it is interesting to hear them clamber around, calling out in the dark, it also leads to a disturbed night's sleep; I wish those returning in the following days a safe and unhindered passage to their homes!

Kittiwake nests in heavy seas at the Wick (Dave Boyle)

It was once again a windy day, and this time the gale had swung round to the south-west so that the Wick offered little shelter. Huge swells of spume-flecked, marine-blue water channelled up the inlet, and the Kittiwakes perching low on the cliff-face had to move fast to escape the clawing waves, with any nests built so low wiped away in seconds. As the morning progressed, surveying became impossible. I retired to Bull Hole, where even inside the hide the vibration of the wind and the haze of sea spray made conditions far from ideal for locating eggs. Despite this I managed to get in a good four hours of surveying. Jess visited to check her ringed birds and to chat, and we spent a pleasant few minutes with both shutters of the hide wide open to give us a panorama of white-capped waves, gliding Gannets and the thunderous hammering of the sea against the base of the cliffs. Guillemot life appears to ignore such meteorological variation, although the number of birds present on the ledges seems to vary a little. Their interactions seem unhindered by the swirling wind; only we humans are inconvenienced. Returning to the farm, I detoured along the archaeological path to find more 'Greater' nests and complete my specified sample of 25, before spending the evening hand-washing clothes – a trying part of island life!

10th: I slept well; the Shearwaters were quieter, but in the morning the wind had not lessened and I was unable to survey at the Wick, instead spending the morning at Bull Hole. Here I believe I had seen all but a handful of the eggs that had been laid (the remaining birds were obscured by rocks or other individuals, so it was impossible to confirm if they really had an egg). The eggs of a couple of pairs appear to have been killed by the inclement weather; one obviously became too cold, lying half in a pool of muddy water, while the reason for the abandonment of the second was unclear.

Back at the farm, I spent the afternoon inputting the data from the last few weeks, after tea and chocolate cake with Sue, Jess, Sarah and Maria. Each summer two long-term volunteers are taken on to help on the island and gain conservation experience; one staying through May and June, the other over July and August – Maria is the first of these. A Yorkshire girl with a no-nonsense attitude, she has fitted in quickly; as well as working on the daily round of island tasks, she is painting information boards for the public hides, colourful depictions of the most common species to be seen.

Fuelled by tea and cake, I checked the Wick again, but to no avail; the wind was still strong, and I did not need to trouble the assembled Puffins by encroaching on their ground. On the way to the site I noticed how the fresh green of Bracken was beginning, little by little, to break up the pink-blue sea of Red Campion and Bluebells. The Sea Campion was also starting to go over in some places, but in more exposed positions, such as the rocky outcrops behind Moory Mere hide, it was fully in bloom, so that these miniature hills appeared snow-capped or iced from a distance. From the Wick I walked out to the Mew Stone, hoping to see the newly fledged Ravens that had been reported from the nest there. I found the nest easily enough, but the birds were not around. I was resting comfortably in a rare sheltered spot, and allowed myself to drift off to sleep for a while, with the roar of waves between the island and the Mew Stone resounding below me, Guillemots and Puffins whirring distantly across the waves and Jackdaws foraging on the steep slopes above the cliffs.

On my way back to the farm I paused at Moory Mere hide. The Kittiwakes were gathering nesting material – mud and vegetation from the poolside which they collected in their beaks and then dipped in the pond to fuse it all together. Many of the apparently less experienced birds would carefully collect a full beak-load to carry away, before immediately losing it all by dipping it too far into the water. They are pretty birds, with snow-white heads, black eyes and lemon yellow beaks. Despite lives spent exposed to the extremes of the elements, they appear delicate and refined compared to the gulls they share the pond with.

Leaving the hide, I saw a Moorhen with four tiny chicks: black downy balls scurrying back to their parent through the vegetation with tiny cheeping calls. The evening brought a meal of chicken and pasta cooked by Maria, fresh asparagus left by Tim, garlic bread provided by Sarah and my own contribution of spinach and beans. Another enjoyable island meal, washed down by a Herefordshire dry cider.

11th: Today, the wind finally lessened and moved round to the west, so that I was able to survey Wick 2G and Wick Corner before heading over to Bull Hole, running the gauntlet of day-trippers gathered to watch the Puffins and straggling in twos and threes between the Wick, Skomer Head and my destination. Most such tourists are affable, carrying varying amounts of equipment, from 35mm cameras and picnics to SLRs, tripods and telescopes. In most cases they also keep to the paths, in the still-present British spirit of obeying the rules; as a result, wildlife and people get along pretty well, and the Puffins seem unconcerned by the attention they receive. I had completed my work by four, and spent some time gluing an eye piece back to my binoculars – only a month after it came off! Hopefully the glue will hold.

12$^{th}$: I felt reflective today, somewhat distant from the excitement of the trip ashore, and I sat and watched the waves drift by as we ploughed through a rough sea to Martin's Haven. On the mainland I gave Chris a lift while the others went with Jess. A diversion took us down past the Murco refinery near Milford Haven with its massive towers, complex pipe-work, storage tanks and an acrid, tarry petroleum smell. The usual visit to the supermarket was followed by lunch (all day breakfasts all round) at the Propeller Café, near the runway of Haverfordwest airfield. We ate outside, with helicopters and small planes landing and taking off as a diverting backdrop to our meal.

Tea at the farm, from left to right: Jessica Meade, Chris Taylor, Annette Fayet, Holly Kirk, Sue Williams

Back at North Haven a particularly tame Grey Seal swam close to the landing point, back flipping under the clear water after gazing up at us for a while where we stood on the *Dale Princess*. After a cup of tea back at the farm, I wandered down South Stream to the tranquil bay, where countless Puffins bobbed on the water and the Kittiwakes circled. In the evening sunshine I got some writing done; some thoughts and a poem, almost my first creative work on Skomer and representing my reflections on the beauty of the island and the changing sea, and how all this fits into my own life. Tomorrow creativity will again take second place to science, as the surveying continues.

### *Thoughts on the boat trip to the mainland*

The waves rise and fall, and the marbled sea fills my vision, like the backdrop to a painting awaiting a subject. For all man's efforts it remains empty and vast, each enterprising surge and exhausted hollow on its surface erased by the next without trace of its triumph or failure. A million of these cycles turns, a million million, as far as my eyes can see. Futile to count or analyse things so transient, whose meaning lies in their action as a whole; the sea that rolls the *Dale Princess*, the sea that with its mass of anonymous, transient patterns shapes the rocks and shapes the lives of birds and men alike.

Was E.B. Ford right when he described Sewell Wright's 'adaptive landscape' as just a sea of waves, whose individual contours are passing, shaping only to obliterate, changing without leaving a mark? Erased like the rise and fall of conversation whose warmth or isolated cold in turns is forgotten by the speaker without comment, or regret, or recognition? Or do they leave something behind, a trace of a pattern in the creatures they mould? A residue on which the changing world must build? Then each wave matters, just as words both gentle and harsh matter to those that speak and those that hear, even if their effect goes unrecognised. And memory and trace can be a lonely companion for the mind that holds their mark, when to others the waters wash away the stain of a meaning that was never meant.

If a mark remains, if each wave leaves a trace, what is it that is produced? A view so reliant upon the awkward ground of what has passed that it can only fail against a plan grown new from an empty space? Or can the pattern; fixed, messy, cobbled out of chance events and twists of fate, mistaken feeling, inward thought, find within its complex whole simplicity revealed? Held within the pattern an insight from confusion, rising above the waves to understand why each is remembered, why a fleeting moment, a flash of love, a glint of water that shines for just a second, is not a waste, but can add a tiny fragment to the building shape, whose melancholy shadow is a price that must be paid. The rocks must be eroded by the waves; nothing added, all taken, dragged away to leave an empty imprint. But cliffs and stones are lifeless and their forms and shapes are sculptures of a forgotten past. The living can adapt and build, and through the pain and love that accompanies change we can grow.

## South Stream Cliffs

*The waves find land, and play on rocks*
*In tranquil swirls while Puffins still*
*On sheltered waters wait, and on*
*The point a lighthouse white*
*In evening gloom creates*
*A distant painted backdrop*

*Flowers of thrift are ruffled by*
*A night-time breeze, their*
*Petals touched by passing time*
*While mayweed carpets gather*
*On the yellow lichen rocks and hold*
*The warmth of dying sunshine*

*A chill of spring has found the cove*
*The shadowed shingle beach and cave*
*Whose curving arch supports*
*The birds and holds their eggs*
*And watches with unchanging face*
*The cycles of their lives*

*Alone and pale upon the sky*
*The moon plots out the season's turn,*
*And gazes down with gentle light,*
*A soothing touch and silver glow*
*An ancient face to watch the earth*
*And race the circling stars.*

13<sup>th</sup>: Given the date, it was perhaps unsurprising that the day began with a soaking: as I neared the Wick, a curtain of rain swept in off the sea, lasting long enough to drive me round to Bull Hole and, of course, lifting as I reached the shelter of the hide. The afternoon was more pleasant, and I completed Wick 1G despite the wind and with an audience of Puffins.

The day ended on a special note, as Dave took a group of us down the track from the sales point to the shore, to where, above a narrow cave, Storm Petrels nest in crevices in a rocky wall. Storm Petrels were known to sailors as 'Mother Carey's chickens'; the name possibly a term for a supernatural force of the sea, or deriving from *Mater Cara*, Latin for Mary, mother of Christ. We clambered over seaweed-covered boulders that shone in the light of a waxing moon, gathering in the cave mouth and sitting amongst the rocks to watch the darting silhouettes pass above us. The tiny, sparrow-sized birds flitted like bats across the star-studded sky as we watched from below. Many sailors believed that each of these birds held the soul of a drowned sailor, and, watching their ephemeral, flickering movement, I could understand why.

Storm Petrel (Dave Boyle)

Dave experimented with a bat detector to see if the petrels were using echolocation to navigate the darkened landscape, but there was no reading. We heard calls from their burrows though: low, hard to discern whirring sounds interspersed with short hiccoughs. It was a subtle, secretive sound compared with the jarring shouts of the Oystercatchers that periodically echoed around the bay. Looking upwards from where we sat, the creviced cliffs formed a frame of dark complexity, with the Thrift fanning out from headlands of rock that nosed into a distant, endless sky of pinprick stars. When the time came to head back, I walked ahead of the others, watching the sea that glittered silver under the moon, the island rolling away from me; a massive, dark, undulating form of milky-grey stone and faded turf, the moonlit farm an intricate but tiny human presence, dwarfed by the immensity of the constellations that arched above it.

14th: I was able to get my survey work completed in time to get back to the farm for the FA Cup final; Man City versus Stoke City. Dave came up from North Haven to watch with me, the only other person on the island with much of an interest in football! In the end Man City triumphed – one nil – and were the better side throughout. I had mixed feelings; despite the fact that my mum's side of the family have always been City fans, I would have preferred it if their win had been achieved without the unfair advantage of a billionaire owner. To me the injection of so much cash is questionable in the face of the massive inequality in the world – and destructive to the game. Winning becomes more important than history and tradition; everything can be sacrificed for success.

For tea, Sarah and I ate homemade pizza with Jess and Sue and finished the day with an action movie watched on a laptop in our lounge. Tomorrow my friends Sarah and Steve are visiting, which I am looking forward to; I was disappointed that the northerly winds had prevented their visit today… and the chance for a meal out on the mainland for me!

15th: I woke early to survey my Wick sites in time to return to the farm and meet Sarah and Steve off the twelve o'clock boat. At the same time Sarah, the assistant warden, was leaving the island for a week, so I will have the flat to myself for a few days. I spent an enjoyable day with my friends, showing them my Guillemot sites (Sarah even managed to see an egg through the 'scope), the Amos and Skomer Head. It was really good to catch up with them, and as their boat pushed out into North Haven in the afternoon sunshine I felt home-sick for Aberystwyth, despite the sun and the rafts of Puffins bobbing on the quiet waters of the bay.

16th: Again I managed to finish my survey work relatively early; most birds at Bull Hole had an egg now, so there was less need to wait for them to reveal whether they were incubating, at least until they neared their expected hatching dates. I walked down to North Haven to get some figures that Tim had requested and spent the afternoon working on those. In the evening I joined the others for Rabbit stew, the Rabbits freshly shot on the island by Dave the day before. It was a delicious meal; Sue cooked the meat in a cider sauce with onions, accompanied by mashed potato and celeriac. I was tired however and, with so many people gathered, struggled to get involved in the conversation, in the end glad to get back to the flat and turn in for the night.

17th: After a restless night's sleep, my mood was softened by listening to an album by 'Love' that Sue had lent me (in return

I lent her my John Martyn CD). Although they have the jangly sixties sound, their music has an edge, hinting at the darker side of a lifestyle that inspired so much colourful music. Rarely for me I had my MP3 player on as I walked along the path to Moory Mere, the west coast sound oddly complementing my progress along the winding path, through the swathes of Red Campion, past the stone walls, with the sea and the land silent behind my wall of sound, as if I was an actor being followed through my daily routine in the opening credits of a film.

After my surveying I had a run; I will need a lot more practice to beat the Skomer record of 23 minutes for a lap of the whole island: it took me 27 minutes to complete a circuit from the farm to Skomer Head, round via the Wick to North Haven and back. But the exercise was strenuous enough to break through my bad mood, and I was able to enjoy an evening meal of sausage and mash followed by birthday cake for Sue, afterwards doing crossword puzzles with Sue, Jess, Maria and John, the spider expert.

John is an interesting character; some of the others find him difficult to get on with, but I have quite a bit of sympathy with him. Sometimes conversation on the island can be a bit over-paced and competitive, while John is slower and more careful in his choice of words. After speaking to him, I am keen to get out one evening and watch the Scarab beetles. He says these creatures are responsible for the tiny holes in the sandy soil of the paths to the Garland Stone and Moory Mere. At night they emerge to collect Rabbit dung, which they pull down into their burrows. The dung serves as a food source for the young beetles as they emerge from their eggs, laid up to a foot under the ground. His research is a reminder that the island is not a single world at the scale of humans and birds, but carries on its back and under its skin cycles of all scales and types, each in its turn intricate and sophisticated.

18th: Today I had a lie-in until nine, just giving myself a half day off this week as I need to survey Bull Hole this afternoon. I was considering a series of sketches I wanted to produce in which different species are portrayed as an integrated part of the landscape, culminating in a self portrait in profile with my face merging into rock, like the profile of the face formed naturally by the cliffs near the Amos. Considering the project, I realised it showed an adaptation of the landscape to fit the character of the organisms that inhabited it, while the evolutionary process represents the adaptation of organisms to the landscape. But, of course, the process goes both ways; the feedback between organism and environment (illustrated so elegantly by Lovelock in *Daisy World*) culminates in our human capability to remain the same while arranging the world to fit ourselves.

I spent the morning creating two of the sketches – one of a Puffin integrated into a coastal scene, and my own profile moulded into a cliff-face; both traced from photos and then adapted. In the afternoon I surveyed Bull Hole before sleeping for a while on the grass just below the hide, the breeze for once light enough for me to drift comfortably with the chorus of Guillemots and Kittiwakes providing the customary island lullaby of raucous cries. Around five, I met Jess and Robin for a swim in North Haven (seeing Robin in a heavy wetsuit, I have to admit feeling a little pride in the fact that I was braving the bay in just my shorts!). Jess and I made it out to the nearest buoy in the bay, plying our way through the icy waters among the Puffins. In the evening I enjoyed a quiet meal and the Europa League final, glad of an hour or two alone. At nine, Jess and Maria came over to watch *The Apprentice* (which they find un-missable) and a relaxed day drew to its close.

19th: I awoke with my head full of ideas, on scientific thought, morality and trust, and scribbled down the best before heading down to the Wick. The vegetation was taller now, the Red Campion above waist height in places, vying with the Bracken for light, the Bluebells in retreat. Much of the Bracken appeared scorched by the prolonged spell of dry weather, and I wondered whether its clonal reproduction is limiting its genetic diversity and potentially leaving it vulnerable to environmental variation. It would be interesting to map its spread and health over time.

In terms of the island as a whole, a revealing endeavour would be to map the vegetation; more clearly here than anywhere I have been previously, it is divided into well-defined patches of different species. Walking towards the Wick from Moory Mere, for example, the Bracken, Red Campion and Bluebell give way to Common Sorrel and grass in a swathe along the valley bottom to the cliffs, where, beyond the path, it is also replaced by the springy snowfall white of Sea Campion. Apart from detecting changes in the environment and the associations between plant communities and animal activities, such a survey might be of historical interest: for example, areas of Elder, Nettles and Bramble might indicate raised nutrient levels around ancient settlements or in areas where livestock were once kept. Here on Skomer the wealth of data on animal and human use of the environment might usefully be augmented by a comprehensive review of the flora.

At the Wick I was able – at last free of the gusting wind that has blown constantly for weeks – to refine my AOT photographs for a couple of tricky sections at Wick Corner and 1G. After the daily visit to Bull Hole, I was back at the farm by four to do some washing and to take our rubbish out to the oil drum for burning, watching over the flames like someone who, in a state of emotional upheaval, burns the evidence of a previous life. Satisfied that the island was not likely to be set alight, I returned to the farm.

This evening Linda Norris put on an exhibition of her pictures painted on Skomer during the week in the old warden's cabin, complete with jazz, wine and cheese. Linda, one of the overnight guests, is married to a previous warden, Denbigh; it is his name spelt out in pebbles on the paving at North Haven, marking the completion of his 23-minute run around the island, including South Plateau. The couple live in the Presellis now, and Linda is an artist having studied fine art at Aberystwyth. She is interested in the use and origins of natural pigments and told me the story of 'ultra-marine' which, before it could be artificially created, was extracted from a single mine in Afghanistan and used in many famous works of art. Some of her pictures really captured the sense of colour and movement in the landscape; sea, sky, flora smeared into near-abstract shapes that captured the feel of the place well. Impressive work from just one week, and I am somewhat chastened by my own meagre accomplishments. The remainder of the evening was taken up making a stir-fry for Sue, Jess and Maria and, although it was not the best I have ever made (I can to some extent blame small pans and limited ingredients), we had a good night.

20th: After the usual round of Guillemot surveys, I walked down to North Haven to find some of the Fulmar-monitoring plots. These birds nest in crevices and ledges scattered over cliff-faces and scree slopes, so that when counting occupied sites you need to move around to see individuals in the deeper declivities. At North Haven, one bird was only visible from one angle from which its head was framed in the mouth of a burrow it had selected as a sheltered spot. The third plot area at North Haven required me to edge out onto a narrow promontory sticking out from the isthmus, looking back to survey the cliff face. It was a little unsettling to be sitting overlooking the turquoise waters and pebble beach of the haven on one side, while close behind the croaky calls of Fulmars echoed upwards from a cliff-face only a foot away in the other direction. It was a privileged vantage point though, made more special by the hazardous approach.

Now I made my way onto the Neck, almost an island in its own right but for the narrow land bridge of the isthmus. Bracken and faded Bluebells covered the ground, mounds of white Sea Campion at the fringes. The paths here are indistinct; only researchers are allowed onto this area of the island, and you feel a certain isolation as you walk away from North Haven. My adventure on this outcrop of rock and birds and flowers did not go entirely to plan; the map I had was unclear, and I strayed beyond my plots at Matthews Wick to Amy's Reach further to the east (the inlet apparently named after a goat that escaped its herders and reached this inaccessible spot before being recaptured!). Here there were no obvious paths, and the dry weather and increased Rabbit activity made the ground a minefield of Manxie burrows, in some places so densely packed that no passage through seemed possible. I continued slowly, at every step expecting to put my foot through a burrow roof, 'Lessers' shouting and swooping around me as I passed their nests scattered in the Bracken. Ravens 'cronked', their hoarse calls carried on the breeze from the pale rocks above the inlet, and the sun was low over the Skomer 'mainland' as I tried in vain to locate my plots.

Eventually I conceded defeat, and so began a slow, hesitant journey back over the uneven terrain. Twice my foot collapsed an occupied burrow. It is disconcerting to reach down through the dusty soil and find a warm, smooth-feathered Shearwater amongst the remains of its burrow roof. Once the earth is lifted, they scuttle into an undamaged part of the tunnel, and repairs can begin. Not having a plank or rock at hand (the ideal replacement roof) I used a criss-cross of Bracken capped by soil from the broken roof and more Bracken on top to make a sturdy, and hopefully fairly waterproof, replacement. I was relieved when I eventually regained the path at the isthmus and returned to North Haven where Ben and Annette had some left-over chilli to sate my hunger, it being well after seven. Apparently there was a 'storm' coming, which on the island consists of any weather accompanied by boat-stopping high winds, and plans were being made for overnight visitors to leave first thing in the morning.

Ben told me that, for the first time, they have managed to track a Shearwater through its entire 'Exodus' journey (their term for the trip the female makes to find different food sources as she grows her egg within her body). Apparently the tracked bird travelled round southern Ireland and up the west coast, before moving south and west out into the Atlantic, eventually returning after two weeks. The contrast in the imagination between a creature making such a long flight over the open sea and the small, quiet birds I had dug from their burrows earlier was striking. Such a local, mundane encounter under the warm, homely earth of Skomer compared with the image of a bird for which the desolate empty waves of the ocean apparently held no foreboding or anxiety. And with all the strength and human power we hold, such a change in lifestyle and environment, such an effort, would be incredible to imagine undertaking.

The 'otherness' of such creatures and the hopeless inadequacy of our persistently anthropocentric appraisal of their behaviour are clear. We can track them and collect facts, but we cannot understand their perspective; to them the fantastic is mundane, if it is anything at all in terms of consciousness. Their unworldly calls that, as I write, fill the stormy night outside these walls are not lost and desperate in the storm, they are not strange or supernatural. They are functional, in their element, without the human emotions we place on them; just as the howling gale represents only shifting air pressures, but can fill us with loneliness or fear, or exhilaration with its power and unpredictability. With our imagination we colour a world where we would love to have those colours, those personalities, those reasons, those emotional patterns. There is a need in us to reach out, to be part of the story, even if it can frighten us and hurt us; we need to understand, not just to know.

21$^{st}$: The promised windy weather prevented any work at the Wick, and I took the opportunity to continue my Fulmar survey at the Basin. The first plot required me to follow the path out towards the Amos, picking my way down until I could look over at the research hide, with the narrow inlet from the Basin below, the Amos and the open sea to my right, and Tom's House behind me. Here Razorbills and Fulmars were almost in touching distance, observing my movements as I scrambled to a good vantage point, doing my best not to disturb their comings and goings. Then I contoured back round to the hide to observe the cliff-face below my initial position. Puffins and Razorbills looked down on me from rough, lichen-feathered rocks, and I took some photos; I could almost capture them in flight as they were held up by the wind, the black, guano-stained ledges of the Amos behind them and the sea surging into the arms of the rocky inlet in a seething chaos of white and ultramarine. After a refreshing couple of hours I headed back to the farm for lunch before visiting Bull Hole. I had tea with Sue, Maria and her boyfriend Chris, as well as Chris, the warden; an Indonesian curry with mixed vegetables and spring greens.

22nd: Again the weather was too windy to survey at the Wick, so I headed straight to Bull Hole. The north coast was wild, the sea, though spattered with white, was still turquoise under blue skies. At Bull Hole, the waves were breaking spectacularly against the foot of the cliffs, the spray rising high enough to leave momentary rainbows in the morning sunshine before falling back. I wrote a description of the scene before checking the birds:

'From Bull Hole I am looking out over a turquoise sea, contoured by massive solid waves, each rolling slow at its base, frantic at its foaming tip, the skin of the ocean disintegrated by capillaries of snowy-white. The base of the cliff shines darkly where the waves surge, their lazy progress exploding upwards as they are smashed into a fountain of diamonds. In slow motion they fall back and in the morning sun leave rainbows fading and still in the air, as rivulets of water pour from the rocks, and the turquoise waves are turned pure white. Above, the Guillemots preen, Kittiwakes glide. A Great Black-backed Gull sits on its nest below the hide, black and white against lichen-yellow rocks. Only the bobbing of Thrift flowers and the shivering grass show the force of the wind, only the majestic scale of the backdrop belies the apparent stillness. Separated by the plywood frame of the hide, I gaze from my empty window and see stillness and movement as one; each crashing wave a part of the flow of the ocean, wrapped around the world as permanent as any rock. The source of change is the one constant, as cliffs crumble, flowers wilt and birds fledge and grow; the chaos of destruction and rebirth is the only lasting thread.'

As yet there are no chicks, and eventually I ventured out of the hide to walk against the wind to the Amos. Here I deposited my bag and 'scope by the path and followed the stream, past Field Forget-me-not, Silverweed, Creeping Buttercup and the ubiquitous Red Campion to Tom's House and my Fulmar plot. The rocky mass of Skomer Head protected the inlet from the wind, and it was warm and sunny in the cove where I sat, the stream trickling over the rocks into the foam-covered sea. I found my Fulmars, dotted in the crevices of the cliff-face at the back of the Amos, and enjoyed the sun; clearly the surrounding headlands make Tom's House a sun-trap, because here the Sea Mayweed is already in flower, and down on the rocks I found the pink-flowered Rock Sea-spurrey, with fleshy leaves and bright yellow anthers contrasting with its rose-coloured petals. Pleased with finding a new species, I withdrew, somewhat reluctantly, to the path.

At the Wick I met Dave and discussed my failed attempt to survey on the Neck. He agreed to show me the paths to Castle Bay and Matthews Wick, and after lunch I followed him over the narrow isthmus and along traces of survey paths to my plots. After completing the plots I returned, pausing to gaze over the sparkling sea to the dramatic, slanted wedge of the Mew Stone, silhouetted in the evening light. Back at the farm

Maria had made us all a sausage bake with mash. Another filling meal and welcome after a day out in the wind.

23rd: The morning was grey, and the winds even higher. Buffeted by the howling north-westerly, I reached Bull Hole and surveyed with the hide shaking and creaking alarmingly around me. On my return journey I watched long, heavy waves driving in from the Irish Sea, hitting the Garland Stone with enough force that the spray and mist of the breakers crested its summit. I learnt later that the BBC team (on the island in preparation for the forthcoming *Springwatch* programme) had made it over on a single lunchtime boat, North Haven offering just sufficient shelter for the *Dale Princess* to come in, although apparently they struggled to keep the boat against the jetty for unloading (she comes in 'nose first' to the landing steps and is held against tyres flung over the concrete platform by the force of her engines; difficult in a heavy swell).

The *Dale Princess* at the landing (Chris Taylor)

After lunch the weather began to clear; I entered some data and worked on the Guillemot statistics until the rain passed, before making my way to the sheltered south of the island to survey the Kittiwakes at High Cliff. It is not an easy colony to monitor, with the viewing position a long way from the cliff-face. The plot areas are large, and on the first visit each nest position has to be recorded. A second visit a few days later records any extra nests, and then fortnightly surveys are carried out to check clutch and brood sizes, and ultimately fledging success. Today the work was frustrating; the photos of the plot were old and had been taken in strong morning sunshine; the late afternoon light picked out different crevices and patterns. As a result, matching nest sites to positions on the photo was laborious. My aim of surveying South Stream cliffs the same evening was thwarted, and I returned home to a quiet tea, television and sleep.

24th: This morning the winds had at last dropped away enough for surveying at the Wick, and Maria joined me so I could train her up to cover my work when I have days off. It was a bit of a relief to have some help, and she was able to complete one of the Kittiwake plots for me in the morning. While she returned to the farm for lunch, I headed round to Bull Hole, stopping at the Amos on the way. Unfortunately my plan to check the Basin Fulmars was spoilt as I had brought out the wrong set of photos, but I had an enjoyable lunch sitting out in front of the research hide in the sunshine.

Later in the afternoon I surveyed one of the South Stream Kittiwake plots, but again it was a painful process. I found Dave there, searching the cliffs for ringed Kittiwakes (and as I approached, taking a nap in this sheltered spot!). He pointed out a bird that had been ringed in France, still with juvenile plumage, asleep in the afternoon sunshine. Again my plot photo took around three hours to fill out, and the shadows were lengthening as I left the tranquil inlet and the cries of the Kittiwakes, and walked over to North Haven to make my second visit to the Fulmar plots. This task was much easier, with many fewer birds and the majority of sites unchanged. The only danger is missing some of the more hidden birds. Shouting down to me from the office, Chris invited me in for tea; an interesting combination of fish pie and sausage sandwich, washed down with a refreshing bottle of Peroni. In North Haven, Iolo Williams and a *Springwatch* cameraman were snorkelling with the Puffins, and we watched them from the balcony, black dots amongst the rafts of birds as they rose and fell on a gentle swell.

25th: Wednesday, and my day off has come around again, the weeks passing quickly with the cycles of surveying and island routines. After some uncertainty the boats did run, and I left at nine with Annette who was on her way back to France for an interview; she is hoping to get funding for a PhD on Puffins and Shearwaters, which would allow her to continue on Skomer for another three seasons. Our conversation on the boat was periodically interrupted by a dousing with seawater as the *Dale Princess* rolled across Jack Sound on a choppy sea, and only when we reached Martin's Haven did we gain shelter from the stiff sea breeze. Annette manages to maintain an unruffled elegance whatever the conditions, and a passer-by watching her walk up from the bay would not have guessed at our rough crossing! As usual I was struck by the lush greenery of the mainland; Cow Parsley is out in the hedgerows, the shining leaves and yellow-green umbels of Alexanders, and where there are dry stone walls of bleached Pembrokeshire rock English

Stonecrop is in bloom, its flowers tiny white stars amongst fleshy red bead-like foliage.

I agreed to drop Annette off in Milford Haven to catch her train and enjoyed the freedom of driving along the winding roads of the peninsular, with summer green all around, still touched by the freshness of spring. Milford Haven is a striking town; from the station where I left Annette, the harbour and various warehouses and quayside apparatus lie just over the road, with the sturdy ironwork of large fishing trawlers and merchant ships somehow incongruous alongside the terrestrial scene of roundabouts, supermarkets and houses.

The main road takes you up a steep hill to a wide, upward-sloping main street, with shops to the left and a narrow parkland to the right, curtailed by an apparently sudden drop, so that from the road the vastness of the bay and its moored tankers are a part of the otherwise typical picture of a small town high street. To me this was a lonely scene; the scale of the sea, the ships and the refineries all seemed to drain the meaning from individual lives. They dwarf the day-to-day scene while keeping our cosy existence ticking over with a massive, damaging, industrial effort. It was like sitting in a house where the walls have been stripped on one side to reveal the wires and pipes beneath. I was pleased to get over to Haverfordwest, fulfil my supermarket requirements – that industrial effort again – and wander around the town.

After taking my normal cut by the church under the Limes and Horse-chestnuts, I explored the upper slopes of the valley in which the town lies. I passed tennis courts and a bowling green, the air full of the nostalgic summer scent of cut grass from where the groundsman was cutting the lawn. Eventually I found a lane that headed downwards to a wooded gully; I passed a large house with a board advertising 'Farm Fresh Eggs' and realised that the spread of new housing around Haverfordwest had left pockets of countryside close to its centre. They had no doubt been saved by the uneven steepness of the valley escarpment. As I turned left down into the woodland, the light under the trees was soft and dappled; Enchanter's Nightshade, Cow Parsley and Wood Avens flowered, and the smell of Wild Garlic lingered even as the plants themselves gave way to denser summer vegetation. The scene was, to me, evocative of many past summers, country walks, childhood, and I was elated and almost overwhelmed by the richness of the experience, more used now to the wide vistas and sweeping, bare country of Skomer.

I emerged from the wood onto a narrow lane by the river, and opposite me was a gateway into the riverside fields and the remains of an old priory. I walked among the ruins, which were peaceful despite the closeness of the new road that stalked across the river on concrete stanchions; it was shielded from the rural, medieval lines of the church by poplar and willow. On the uphill side of the site were a mix of sheltering trees, a sloping grazed field accessed through an iron kissing gate, and the long grass, Yellow Flag Iris, Germander Speedwell and Creeping Buttercups of a marshland. I saw two Common Blue butterflies flitting through the grasses and wandered around an area of cultivated beds of thyme, chives, mint and lavender. Eventually it was time to walk back along the river into the town and The Georges for lunch: gammon and turkey pie and chips, eaten outside in the company of a Robin, which perched close on the table and hopped around expectantly until I gave in and threw him a bit of a chip. I read for a little while in the quiet garden, then returned to the car; due to the rough seas I had to be back early for the boat.

In the end I arrived at Martin's Haven in good time. Kenny had caught Mackerel and sat in the door of the wheelhouse gutting the fish and throwing the entrails out to a flotilla of circling gulls. Five or six slender-winged, cream-headed Gannets flew with them and, on seeing the fish, would spear down amongst their competitors, taking the food from the 'Lessers', disappearing briefly under the waves like white darts, then bobbing up to swallow their catch in the wake of the boat. In the evening Maria made a potato and leek soup, and our meal was followed by the traditional crossword or two from Jess's cache before I turned in for an early night in preparation for a new week of surveying.

26th: At the moment there is a lot happening on the island, mostly centred round the activities of the *Springwatch* team. Tim Healing, among many other things an expert on the Skomer Vole, is here to do some trapping and for an interview with Iolo. He has many stories to tell; talking with him yesterday evening, I was interested by all the unknowns surrounding this vole. Why does their rate of breeding fall at low population levels and increase, counter-intuitively, at high? What drives the fluctuations in populations? Are factors such as disease or parasitism at work?

For all the focus on the seabirds and their ecology, the Skomer Vole is the only endemic subspecies on the island, and in some ways its needs may be somewhat at odds with those of other species. For example, according to Tim, Skomer Voles prefer dense, tall Bracken, without an understory of other plants that allows them to move easily under cover from predators. The Skomer Vole is also one of the very few mammals that can eat Bracken despite the carcinogens it contains; this may indicate resistance to the various toxins or be explained by the lifespan of the vole (around two years) which may be too short for long-term damaging effects to build up. These voles are 50% larger than the mainland Bank Voles from which they vary and are relatively easy to handle, being adapted to avoid aerial predators by 'freezing' rather than terrestrial predators, best avoided by fast movement but absent from the island. Apparently the island's shrews may also be genetically distinct from their mainland cousins, with paler fur and white ear tufts.

In more general terms I was interested to hear that Tim and other researchers have indeed surveyed the vegetation types on the island, as I had been considering. It is good to know that the various parts of the ecological jigsaw of Skomer have all been given some attention, even if, as Tim says, we know much of what happens here, but often little about why it happens.

Against this backdrop of activity surveying continues. This morning I escaped the *Springwatch* team who had crowded into our kitchen for a brew before filming (too many people to be polite to first thing!) and initially walked to the Wick, which was once again too windy to survey, and then to the Amos to check the Fulmar plots. Jess arrived while I was surveying the first plot and we had coffee and biscuits, me leaning outside the hide as if waiting at a roadside kiosk for my morning cuppa; a strange scene with the rocks dotted with Puffins and Razorbills all around us and the surging sea below.

Eventually I walked around to the Amos path to complete my survey of the cliff-faces, finishing by scrambling down to the rocks by Tom's House, again finding myself reluctant to leave this warm, sheltered spot, the mesmeric crashing waves and the feeling of being separated from the rest of the world by the arms of rock and turf that bound the inlet. After surveying Bull Hole and a quick lunch, I walked to North Haven to re-check the Fulmar plots on the Neck. I managed to find the paths Dave had shown me and to wend my way through the fresh green Bracken, Bluebells and shouting gulls to the cliffs. At Castle Bay three Seals surfaced in the calm, clear water; the sound of their exhalations echoed around the cliff-faces of the narrow inlet, round heads shining and wet, apparently content to simply observe the scene, unhurried and relaxed. In the evening Sue made a tasty curry with rice, lentils cooked in garlic and spices and mackerel; a good way to end the day.

27th: As the wind had finally dropped, I determined to complete the nest mapping of the Kittiwakes at all the Wick plots and spent the day on the cliffs, finally leaving, tired but glad to have achieved my goal, at around four. I surveyed Bull Hole and walked back along the north coast in an exuberant mood with my work done, listening to The Waterboys (*Fisherman's Blues*) on my MP3 player and watching the gulls, the tankers moored in the sunshine of the bay, the tarnished grey mat of Bluebells that still hold a kind of beauty in senescence.

Reaching North Valley, the Short-eared Owl hovered close, and I looked up at its pale, ghost-like face and wide powerful wings, thinking that the sight, experienced without knowledge of the bird, would be sinister and perhaps frightening: the flat white mask and staring eyes, the size of the predator. Yesterday the owls were filmed for *Springwatch*. They have a nest, with six chicks, which are fed mainly with Skomer Voles; Tim estimates a pair with young might take up to 300 in a season, a potentially significant number. They hunt low over the open ground of North Valley. If they manage to catch a vole in their powerful talons they return to their nest amid the Bracken, deftly transferring their unfortunate prey from talon to beak mid-flight before they land; an impressive bird to be living on the doorstep of the farm.

28th: The day began with driving rain crossing the island, carried by a strong north-westerly wind, and I took refuge in Bull Hole hide. My reward: the first chick I have seen. Moving the 'scope up to site 169 at the top of the survey area, I saw fragments of turquoise eggshell on the narrow ledge. Then, as the adult sheltered its tiny charge, the last of the shell was cast off, and the black downy chick, hardly able to stand, was enveloped beneath the white breast feathers of its parent. A cheerful moment under clearing skies; by lunchtime the improving weather allowed me to move to Wick Corner and to survey the Kittiwakes at South Stream cliff. Here, the vegetation that tumbles with the stream onto the dark rocks had become deep and lush; banks of Hemlock Water Dropwort, the purple flowers of Bittersweet in the shady nooks, Nettles, waist-high Red Campion and Bracken. Amongst this sea of greenery the Sedge Warblers fluttered with chattering, churring calls.

The sloping bands of rock that form South Stream cliff support several groups of Guillemots, lined up on guano-whitened horizontal ledges, and the Kittiwake nests are dotted between these. Occasionally their nests also occur in rows along a ledge, but they are much more distantly separated from each other than the Guillemot territories. Each bird sits on a built-up mound of mud and vegetation, topped by the bowl of the nest which is flattened by its owner's feet. Some already guard brown-grey eggs, revealed as the birds adjust their position. I was reluctant to leave the peaceful bay and sat for a while on the rocks, watching Razorbills and Guillemots rise and fall with the navy blue waves, while Puffins whirred over my head. Far beyond the shelter of the cliffs giant waves silently battered the coast of Skokholm.

Skomer Vole

Back at the farm I had an early tea before accompanying Tim, Sue and some of the overnight guests, as Tim checked his vole traps. As I have described, the Skomer Vole is a lot larger than its mainland counterpart and lives amongst the extensive stands of Bracken on the island. There is a high-density population in North Valley, and it is probably not a coincidence that the nest of the Short-eared Owls is close by! The trapping plot for Skomer Voles is a grid about half a hectare in area, marked out by regularly positioned poles. These poles also indicate where the Longworth live mammal traps have been placed.

According to Tim, Longworth traps were designed in World War Two when there was an effort to control mouse and rat populations (it was estimated that the equivalent of one in twenty shiploads of grain brought to the UK actually ended up in the bellies of these opportunist creatures). The layout of the traps remains largely unchanged from the original design; there is an entrance tunnel with a treadle that triggers the door of the trap to close behind the animal. This tunnel is fitted into a larger metal box, filled with bedding material and rolled oats or hamster food. The tunnel fits into the main part of the trap at an angle so that any liquid collecting inside will drain out. The only change to the trap over the years has been the addition of a shrew escape hole. These were added as trapping shrews requires a licence under the Wildlife and Countryside Act of 1981. The much smaller shrews need to eat every 20 minutes and, although the traps can be supplied with dog food or fishing castors, they would have to be checked each hour if these tiny mammals were not provided with an escape route.

We spent half an hour walking from cane to cane in the middle of a sea of Bracken and Red Campion, and under a darkening early evening sky, pausing at each trap to check the contents. I had a go at turning the trap upright, taking out the tunnel section (and checking the vole was not hiding inside it, as they sometimes do) and then emptying the main section of the trap into a clear plastic bag. There was the vole, burrowing into a corner of the bag; the idea is to pick them up by the scruff of the neck to avoid being bitten. I was a little too hesitant, concerned not to injure the creature, and Tim finally made the whole thing look easy, expertly gripping the vole behind the neck and pulling it from the bag. It was a female and pregnant; an individual that had been trapped before.

When caught, a tiny metal ear tag is clipped onto the vole, giving it a unique number, and allowing population estimates to be made using the 'Capture – Mark – Recapture' method. A number of voles are trapped (as many as possible) marked and released. In a second round of trapping the proportion of marked animals recaptured is used to calculate the population size. The method is not perfect, and sometimes the number of voles present saturates the available traps. Another problem is bias caused by individual voles becoming addicted to the traps, returning straight to them after release to enjoy a warm place to stay and easy food. We found two voles previously caught during this year's trapping, and several that had been marked last year.

Very few Skomer Voles survive more than two years in the wild, although they can last longer in captivity, free of predation, disease and parasitism. Wild voles are susceptible to ticks, which can be serious given that the animals only have about 3 ml of blood to begin with, and these ticks can also transmit blood parasites. In captivity the rate of red blood cell replacement falls (high rates are caused by an immune response to infection) showing the extent to which these wild voles are fighting disease and parasitism. Incidentally, Tim told me that, as a result of modern living standards and healthcare, the rate of red blood cell production in humans is also low, and compared with tribes of indigenous people in wild parts of the world, our lifespan is also greatly extended. Without all our artificial products a human might expect to live just 25 years; it is no wonder that our bodies, and minds, degenerate as we enter our 60s, 70s and 80s, well beyond our natural life expectancy.

A final observation Tim made fitted well with my previous thoughts on the many scales of life on the island and the miniature landscapes I had imagined. He pointed out that for the Skomer Voles and the other small species on the island, Bracken is the 'dominant tree of a forest landscape'. And, of course, it is the lack of real trees that either draws the eye and the mind outward to the scale of the sweeping plateau, the bird-filled skies, the endless sea and the abstract timelessness that brings one close to our ancestral past, or downwards to the complex mosaic of plants, insects and mammals of quickly changing, interwoven cycles of life and death. Those cycles, that complexity, occur at both scales; it is only relative to our own lives that one appears constant and wide, the other changing and complex. Without trees to bridge the gap between these two worlds they appear separate, distinct, the contrast striking. To me the division seems to reflect the same divide between our pursuit of knowledge and detail, and our understanding of the whole. We feel a need to explore every avenue, to make use of every potential; competing, turning everything to functional purpose, our lives are a stream of constant stimuli without pause. We become enclosed and unable to appreciate the whole, that realm of understanding where patterns are not analysed but recognised in their undissected beauty; where each individual fragment does not have to be pursued and known in a futile spiral of searching; where we can step outside the flow of action and find direction and meaning.

The island is perhaps a parable for that split between science and religion, between functional and spiritual that has arisen over the last century. We have cut down the trees of thought that allowed us to gain an overview, to reach upwards and reflect on our actions from a perspective outside that of our narrow material interest. And now, prevented from achieving that growth, we have to choose between a shrinking world of religious abstraction and a blind competitive fight in which we must take in, process and use every bit of information without reflection, for the sake of what it can gain us, with each gain itself a new stimulus to push further. Personally, that divide, and the meeting point between those different perspectives, is one I see in my own thoughts. The key is to somehow bridge the gap rather than just produce abstract visions that only make us dissatisfied with the competitive world of detail, without offering a real alternative.

29$^{th}$: Today my goal was to complete my early-season Fulmar checks, leaving a week free to concentrate on spotting Guillemot hatchlings at Bull Hole and the Wick. It was a damp, misty morning, and I surveyed Bull Hole first, seeing a second chick. Its small downy form, with pointed beak complete with a white egg tooth (with which it breaks through the egg shell to hatch) appeared for a brief few seconds as its parent changed position. Next I walked over to the Amos and had lunch with Jess, as she too tried to catch a glimpse of an egg or chick between the packed ranks of birds. Again the Fulmars proved a relaxing change from Guillemot observation, a chance to move around and to visit different areas of the island. In the afternoon, fuelled with sponge cake that Maria had spent the morning making, I once more headed over to the Neck and spent an enjoyable afternoon checking Castle Bay and Matthews Wick for more Fulmars. In the evening Sarah and I were joined by Maria, Jess and Sue for wine and cake, and an entertaining end to the day.

30$^{th}$: The day began misty and wet. I saw a flock of around 25 Jackdaws near Bull Hole. In a flurry of corvid activity, a family of five Ravens, fledged recently near the Garland Stone, flew past me along the coast, while a pair of Choughs called out with their distinctive 'chee-ow' from posts around the Rabbit exclosure. There were five more Guillemot chicks at Bull Hole, and I saw one being fed; an adult brought back a shining silver Sprat which was deposited on the ledge for the chick to peck at with its tiny black beak. The youngsters are not entirely black;

they have light chests, and their wings already carry the shadows of the white wing spots of the adults. In some ways they are harder to see in the shadows than the sometimes brightly coloured eggs from which they hatch, especially if the parent is holding them to the side facing away from the hide.

In the afternoon I crossed the island to the Wick via Skomer Head. It is a Bank Holiday, with an extra day boat and therefore an extra fifty people enjoying the island. Almost all stick to the paths while they admire the birds and scenery, but for the field assistant in a hurry to reach his next plot the number of people can sometimes prove a frustration!

I completed Wick 1G and 2G with my usual entourage of Puffins watching from the rocks and hummocks of Sea Campion and creeping around me as I worked. Then, lifting my bag, I watched in horror as my camera rolled from the top of it, agonisingly slowly but inevitably towards the cliff-top and over. Standing, I saw it land on the grass some 20 feet below, bounce out of its case, then fall again onto the slanting rocks above the sea, cartwheeling to a halt just short of the waves. I picked my way down via a narrow fissure in the rocks, convinced it would be smashed. However, despite some dents and a crack in the casing – and once I had replaced the scattered batteries – it still worked! A lucky escape and a new view of the Wick from the shore, showing the slanting plates of volcanic rock close-up with the main cliff-face towering over me across the narrow strip of translucent turquoise water, the cries of Kittiwakes and the chunnering of Guillemots echoing around me, and Puffins looking quizzically down from the cliff-top that I had so suddenly vacated, as if curious about my sudden burst of activity.

31<sup>st</sup>: I was back at the Wick for the morning, surveying Wick Corner. Of all my sites this is closest to the typical image of a seabird colony, with the Guillemots lining a single, deep ledge, a segment of the sandwiching layers of basalt that make up the cliff-face. There are a few slanting, densely packed areas, others (much easier to survey) where there are single lines of white fronts and chocolate brown backs, with occasional galleries of partners crowded in behind their mates. Today I saw the first hatchling for the site, fighting free of the shell of its turquoise life-support; there should be more by my next visit.

After lunch I continued to Bull Hole where I saw many eggs but few new chicks. A pair of Reed Buntings was singing from the willows near the North Stream research path, and there was a hint of real summer warmth rising from the thick vegetation of North Valley. We had a BBQ in the evening, and with the promise of a day off ahead of me I was able to relax and enjoy a bottle of 'Hopping Hare', a light, tasty summer ale, followed by some slightly less exciting cans of John Smiths! After some arguments amongst this week's volunteers and the accompanying stress, everyone needed the chance to have a relaxed evening, and we exchanged stories and banter in front of the old farm house before the chill night air forced us, as always, into the old wardens' cabin. It was a pleasant evening; we were celebrating the birthdays of Lynn, the WT's fundraising officer, extrovert and full of stories, and Hannah, Ben's wife. Ben had made an impressive cake in the shape of a hedgehog, with spiced chocolate spikes; as usual, an evening on the island is not complete without excellent food and the draining of the ubiquitous boxes of red wine.

# *June*

Little Owl

1st: Luckily, given the activities of the previous night, I had the day off today and in the morning did little beyond cooking myself a fry-up and tidying the kitchen. I strolled down to North Haven to print off some work on the Guillemot data. By the track to the office I found Water Mint, Procumbent Pearlwort and Lesser Spearwort. They were growing in a localised wet flush where a stream trickles over the path, little more than a muddy couple of feet along the track. The island flora seems to be characterised by such small patches of diversity, with the majority of the land outside these scattered stands dominated by Bracken, Red Campion, Common Sorrel and Wood Sage.

In the afternoon I hid myself away with *The Moonstone* and my Spanish books at Tom's House. Just above the rocks of the shore there is a soft bed of Yorkshire Fog below a steep section of the slope, and this shelters the spot on the landward side, with the outcrop of the Amos and Skomer Island protecting it to the north and south. The outcome is a warm sunny space to recline, hidden from visitors and protected from the wind, but with a view out over the glittering sea and the crags and natural arch of the Amos. An afternoon of sleeping and reading took me out of the mindset of researcher and observer to the extent that in the evening I was sufficiently detached to write a few lines of poetry.

2nd: Today a heavy mist had rolled in from the sea, and my walk to the Wick had that silent quality of stillness and uncertainty, that soft dampening of senses that fog brings. The tendrils of cloud, waves of twisting white that skimmed the cliff-face, made the familiar site seem wild and mysterious. The mist was light enough for most of the morning to survey my plots and the lack of wind very welcome. Only on a few occasions did the heightening sun catch the droplets of water in the air to create a gold-grey sheen and hide the detail of cliff and birds.

In the afternoon my stint at Bull Hole was punctuated by the boom of the foghorn at South Bishop, sounding its warning to tankers and, by the sight of my regular friend, the Pembroke to Rosslare ferry. The dull thunder of the ferry's engines drifts over the empty sea to my hide twice a day, so that I can detect its approach from at least three or four miles away. Its constancy of route – appearing distantly north-east of Grassholm and slipping between that Gannet-covered rock and Skomer before passing out of sight, or emerging suddenly from beyond the outcrop of Bull Hole cliffs on its outward trip – and its regularity – appearing at about quarter past eleven in the morning and four in the afternoon – are somehow comforting. That reassurance may come from its steady, firm progress, its indication of other lands beyond the horizon, the fact that it carries hundreds of people within its white shell to whom Skomer and its inhabitants raise perhaps a few seconds of curiosity as the island slides by, indistinct and dark, with a skirt of white breakers and a crown of green and grey.

3rd: With little wind and clear skies, today was the first when heat, and not the cold, made surveying at the Wick a little uncomfortable. The summer sun was high above the cliffs by ten o'clock, and the glare made the view through the 'scope hazy and indistinct; I decided to walk around the island to spend the hottest part of the day at Bull Hole, with the cool coast breeze (so recently a subject of complaint) providing respite from the heat of the sun, inescapable on the treeless plateau of the island. I spotted a good number of new chicks in a five-hour stint, at the same time considering my report on the Guillemot productivity data from the last twenty years. The falling productivity levels suggested by the WT data may indicate an increase in egg losses with population size that could offset the benefits of increasing defence from predators. This kind of density dependence would give a 'hump back' productivity curve for a colony as its size and density increased. Large colonies may have a relatively low productivity, remaining intact because the advantages of breeding inside the group still just exceed the dangers of starting a new colony, outside the protection of large numbers of other individuals. I am considering some way of comparing productivity in dense and sparse colony areas, but any effect may be confounded by the different environmental characteristics of different sites, while the number of egg losses may be too low to show significant differences in loss rates.

4$^{th}$: I got up early enough to walk over to the Wick for an eight o'clock start so that I could survey before the glare of the sun obscured my view of the cliff-face. The day began misty and cool, with little wind and an early morning freshness. The air was full of scents: dry turf, the salty smell of the sea, a hint of sweetness from the remnants of the Bluebells. Up until now the strong winds had carried away these scents, or they had been deadened by the dry heat of the sun, a whole aspect of experience that I had been missing. I took it in now as I scanned my sites for new chicks. The sun burnt through the mist to hang in a clear blue sky; by ten the heat and glare were back once more, and I moved to Bull Hole, where six hours of observation took me up to 60 chicks seen. Over such a long period I was able to watch the times when the colony seemed full of life and movement; birds squabbling, preening, swapping position with mates, fussing over a hatching egg, and times when all seems drowsy and sedate in the haze of the mid-afternoon sun, birds sitting tight with head tucked into their wings or standing with their beaks resting on the bird to one side or the other. Waves of movement and calm seem to spread from one area to another, as if the actions of one trigger a similar response in others.

Innate instinct does seem to govern many of the apparently complex behaviours of the Guillemots – just as the pinhead-sized brains of bees can produce amazing complexity and apparent logic in the behaviour of these social insects. It seems – from observations of Guillemot reactions to the unexpected – that at times they are almost mechanically responding to cues and stimuli, producing inappropriate actions when something unexpected occurs; they appear unable to adapt to, or even recognise, obvious deviations from normality. I watched a bird arrive at its ledge with a Sprat, presumably to feed its chick. Receiving no response from its mate, the bird waited, fish in mouth, for a few minutes before placing the Sprat on its mate's back and leaving. There it remained, shining in the sunlight, until the bird on which it rested realised it was there and ate it.

Even more oddly, Jess has seen a bird return with a fish that it proceeded to 'feed' to its un-hatched egg, apparently oblivious to the fact that the chick it had expected had not yet emerged, suggesting that some pre-hatching cue, perhaps the noise of the chick moving in the egg, triggers a parent to bring food. Pairs often continue to behave as if they still have an egg when it has been lost; again apparently demonstrating unconsciously controlled behavioural patterns.

It is interesting that the activities of such a social species, during the breeding season at least, show behaviour that resembles complex human activity, but which on closer inspection may just be a series of innate reactions, triggered without thought. These responses provide the flexibility to survive, breed and raise a chick, but no more; where circumstances move beyond the scope of such basic actions their direction is random, even ludicrous. The limits to the action of selection are shown, the sophistication unmasked as a series of simple reflexes.

5th: This morning there were several new chicks at Wick Corner, taking the site total to 22. I completed the survey early, as Zara, Nick and Brian (old housemates from Aberystwyth) were visiting. It was good to catch up and I gave them a guided tour, including taking them down to South Stream cliffs to watch the Guillemots, Kittiwakes and Puffins. We also saw the Little Owl (after eight weeks my first sighting!) sitting remarkably well camouflaged on the rocks near the trig point, posing for the phalanx of camera lenses trained on it.

It is surprising how photography can move from hobby to something like an obsession. Some photographers will lie over the path at the Wick with cameras and lenses worth thousands of pounds just to get one 'perfect' shot of a Puffin, oblivious to the rest of the island and to any experience of the context in which these birds exist; a context that makes the situation unique, that can bring understanding and a living experience rather than a perfect but lifeless image. I have felt that desire to capture better images myself. Once a Puffin or Razorbill is photographed close-up you begin to want more: a picture of the bird in flight, a certain pose or backdrop, a bird carrying Sand Eels. You can feel that rising drive to get better equipment, to stay longer, to get closer. If not controlled, it is all too clear how an obsession develops, how perspective is lost, how one could pursue forever and still be dissatisfied, as each effort just raises the bar of desire.

Occasionally people become thoughtless of others in their single-minded quest; blocking paths, disturbing birds, encroaching on fragile habitat, just to get the shot they want. The pursuit becomes less a case of artistic endeavour, more a contest. To me that can become an exercise in missing the point, can stop people appreciating things because they do not have the time – the goal, the ambition, the competition is all, the compulsion to capture and keep every experience, despite the fact that in doing so the actual moment is robbed of meaning. The captured image replaces what it should be depicting, the aid to memory becomes the memory itself; the feelings and emotions of the moment are those of getting the shot, not those that define the experience itself as unique, or poignant, or beautiful.

Of course, this obsessive cycle depends on having the money to buy the equipment. If you do not have that equipment, you are forced to see the whole. Although you might miss out on getting the highest quality picture, you gain the opportunity to enjoy the moment for itself and its content. On the other hand, photography can be a powerful way to tell a story or make a point, and many great photographers visit the island – people who treat their skill as an art, not a contest. And for the majority it remains a rewarding and enjoyable hobby; as always the problems come at the extremes. In a unique place like Skomer the people at those extremes are more visible, more starkly contrasted with the enjoyment gained by a child, a family, a couple, seeing such a place for the first time.

After an enjoyable day, Zara, Nick and Brian returned to the mainland; Brian and Zara were somewhat sunburnt after a day on the open, treeless paths! I was a little sad to see them go; it had been good to hear their news of Aberystwyth and to share some of my island experiences.

6$^{th}$: There were enough clouds in the early morning sky over the Wick for me to make a good survey, finding new chicks at Wick 1 and 2G. With every visit I am able to break down the mass of birds more coherently into territories, the mates packed around incubating birds and 'loafers' at the colony edges. As this happens, I become more confident of my early-season definitions of sites: active, regular, those where birds merely loiter. And as I see more chicks, the final stage of the work (following these birds to fledging) comes into view and gives me the final push needed to maintain my efforts. In the evening, Sarah, Maria and Sue were out ringing Shags on Midholm, returning later with the scratch and bite marks to prove it! I had tea with Jess, whose tastes in food are a bit more particular than mine; she had been unimpressed by my use of blocks of tinned ham in a stir-fry when I last cooked. But (with a more careful choice of ingredients) the spaghetti bolognese I made went down much better, and we had a good meal.

7ᵗʰ: The day began with dark clouds of heavy rain racing over the sea and brushing the island, interspersed with periods of sunshine, fleeting rainbows fading over the waves in the wake of the squalls. At Bull Hole, Guillemots huddled with beads of water like pearls dotting their fine water-resistant feathers, edging away from pools of muddy water forming on the wider ledges. Returning to Wick Corner in the afternoon, I was able to make a reasonable survey; the light was good, but a gusting wind made the task harder. Three chicks had been lost from the front row of birds that line the almost continual single ledge of the plot. I learnt that evening that a boat had come into the inlet and a diver had retrieved buoys from the shore below. This disturbance had flushed birds from the ledges and most likely caused these losses, either as a result of the chicks falling from the ledges in alarm or being picked off by gulls while the adults were absent. Day visitors got photographs of the boat and it was reported, hopefully preventing any more disturbances.

In the evening we had a meal in the old farm to celebrate the birthday of one of this week's volunteers, Jane. Everyone provided a dish with a very loose Indian theme, and we ate well before crowding into our lounge to watch *Springwatch*; surreal to be seeing the scene at North Haven live on TV while being so close to it. We talked and shared drinks until finally turning in around midnight; tomorrow I have a day off, and a trip to Haverfordwest beckons.

8<sup>th</sup>: It was a blustery, cloudy morning as I crossed Jack Sound on the *Dale Princess*, looking forward to seeing how summer was progressing on the mainland. On the Cardiganshire banks by the road from Martin's Haven the dusty blue flowers of Sheep's Bit Scabious were in bloom in places, and by the gateway to West Hook Farm (guarded by two stone Puffins adorning the tops of the gateposts) the banks held the stacked yellow inflorescences of Common Toadflax, each pale yellow flower with orange lip and long spur – dramatic and beautiful. In Haverfordwest, and after the usual trek around the supermarket, I had a short stroll through the woodland lining the steep valley escarpment. The Cow Parsley that had dominated a couple of weeks ago was now pale and yellowed, dying back to make room for a verdant tide of Red Campion, Wood Avens and Broad-leaved Dock, shaded by the darkening green leaves of Sycamore, Ash and Wych Elm. Bird song echoed under the cavernous, arching branches burdened with foliage, and two or three immature Wrens fluttered up from the path ahead of me, still uncertain on their wings.

Eventually I emerged from the peace of the wood and had lunch at The Black Sheep, choosing fish and chips, simple but with tarragon batter around the pollock and a tasty Tartar sauce. I managed to jot down some thoughts that had been circling my head over the previous few days before visiting the Oxfam Bookshop, buying a couple of Spanish language books and picking up Miles Davis's *Kind Of Blue* from the music shop, as recommended by the owner.

As the weather had worsened during the day, I was forced back early to Martin's Haven and the boat home. I stood wedged in the cabin doorway with waves slamming over the bow as we crossed Jack Sound, the boat – which suddenly seemed a lot smaller – corkscrewing across the channel. It was not a bad crossing for the experienced boatmen, but it was exciting for me. Carl and Kenny were talking about a day when the boat rolled over so far that, if you lay down in the back, you could look down at your feet above the waves. A sturdy vessel, the *Dale Princess* was built in 1981 but gets a refit every year that keeps her in good shape for daily work.

9th: My usual survey round of the Wick and Bull Hole was successful and positive, with new chicks at the Wick and 109 in total now at Bull Hole. Later in the day I surveyed the Kittiwakes at High Cliff. With the new photographs it was a much easier task than on my previous visit, and I found a more comfortable spot from which to view the plots, in a natural depression between the rocks. South Stream cliff dropped away behind me, 'Lessers' settling back on to the rocky pavement of the cliff top from where I had disturbed them a few moments before. Guillemots and Puffins dotted the sea, their paths criss-crossing the evening sky below and around me. It was warm and I was sheltered from the wind, with high white cloud softening the sunlight, so that I was able to get a clear view of the birds.

Almost all the nests were occupied by a single adult, sleeping or adjusting their carefully constructed solid nests, built up from the ledges like ceremonial pyres or convex-peaked ants' nests. The scene was quiet and organised in contrast to the noisy jostling and squabbling of the Guillemot colonies, like an estate of detached houses compared to the hectic campsite of a summer rock festival. As the sun began to fall in the west, I headed back to the farm, where Jess made tea for me and Sue: pasta with tomato sauce, after a starter of fresh asparagus tips in butter, all washed down with a glass of real ale.

10th: It seems unbelievable that I have been on the island for eight weeks now; I am halfway through my contract already. The island itself has changed with the passing weeks. Where the path to the Garland Stone had crossed a carpet of iridescent Bluebells it is now surrounded by their straw-coloured flattened stems, grey remnants of flowers and masses of green seedpods. In North Valley swathes of Creeping Forget-me-not fill the stream bed where the path crosses it, but they are crowded by a forest of Hemlock Water Dropwort with its umbels of tiny white flowers, dotted on warm days by shining blue and green flies that feed on its nectar.

The Whitethroats and Sedge Warblers are now hidden by the fully leaved Goat Willow and, walking from the stream to the farm, there are purple and white-flowered Marsh Thistles, tall Bracken, Red Campion and just short of the ruined outbuildings a small stand of Common Figwort. Where the various island streams – mere trickles after the dry weather – reach the coast, they are shrouded in sheltered spots by scrambling Bittersweet and Hemlock Water Dropwort, in more open areas running past mats of Silverweed and patches of Creeping Buttercup. Sea Mayweed is in bloom, with its large daisy flowers, white and yellow, like fried eggs, fleshy leaves forming soft clouds on the rocks of the shore. There are more Rabbits (they have eaten a patch of Gypsywort growing in South Stream that I had hoped to see flower) and the paths are scattered with Shearwater wings, the sole remnants of predation, joined by delicate light bones and called 'angel wings' by some people, a phrase I find somewhat macabre.

Against this changing backdrop, my surveying routine at the Wick and Bull Hole continues. This afternoon I completed the second South Stream Kittiwake observations and saw my first Kittiwake chick of the season, downy and white with black beak and legs, almost as delicate in its colouring as the adult birds, like a child's interpretation of a chick. As always, the scene at South Stream was peaceful and relaxing. I managed to find a spot where I could sit between the blocks of basalt and observe the cliffs from a bed of Sea Mayweed, the stream trickling over the rocks close by. The day was rounded off by a meal of steak (bought from a local butcher by Sue) homemade chips, tomatoes, onions, mushrooms and pepper sauce. The flavours and amount of crispy fat made it the best food I've had so far on the island.

11<sup>th</sup>: I woke early and spent the day surveying my Guillemot sites and completing the Kittiwake plots at the Wick, finishing the day in the evening sunshine surrounded by Puffins gathered for their evening soirée. In the soft light many drowsed on dried cushions of Sea Campion, while others stood and surveyed the hillside, occasionally stretching and flapping their short wings before resuming their vigil. Some were more active, scurrying over the mounds of browning vegetation to dive into their burrows with beaks full of shining Sand Eels. I returned to the farm via the Amos, seeing the family of five Choughs that have recently fledged from a nest near the Basin. They were gathered close at the end of North Wick Ridge, rising with their characteristic 'chee-owing' call to glide and swerve through the sky above me, over the shoulder of the nearest headland and out of sight. The evening was spent watching Clint Eastwood's *Gran Torino*, his last film as an actor, and in its own way as good and striking as *Unforgiven*.

12th: During the night heavy cloud and strong winds brought much needed rain to the island, although it was much less appreciated when seeping under our front door and across the kitchen floor! I took the opportunity to input my Guillemot data from the last few weeks and to think about ways to test the effect of position in the colony on breeding success. In the afternoon I walked out to Bull Hole; low clouds raced over the plateau so that the outcrops of rock on the north coast were pale and mysterious amidst a cloak of rain. In the shelter of the hide I listened to the patter of rain, blown on a swirling wind in staccato bursts, and watched the impervious Guillemots continue life as normal. Survey completed, I returned to make a moussaka for a shared meal in the old farm to celebrate another volunteer's birthday. It was well received and I enjoyed a couple of bottles of real ale, a light summer beer called 'Wychcraft' and a Banana Bread beer that Dave certainly didn't appreciate. I am undecided myself, but one is probably enough for an evening.

13th: Despite the drinks last night, I managed to get down to Wick Corner by nine. The fog that had drifted around the farm the night before was gone, the air clear and fresh, with the headlands, fields and hills of Pembrokeshire colourful and detailed, not faint ghosts of shape in the mist. The sky was a mass of rounded grey clouds. Only out to sea was their cover lightened, and they became smooth and high, fading into pale blue above Grassholm. As I walked down the High Park path, the clouds, the smell of wet earth and the edge of cold reminded me of childhood holidays, oddly evoking summer in a way no amount of sunshine can, and making me feel alert and positive without the tiring lethargy that can smother the mind on a hot day on the treeless island. Sitting behind my 'scope at the Wick, I was investigated by a particularly curious Puffin, scuttling over to watch me watch the Guillemots, standing on my clipboard and looking at me with head on one side when I glanced down. These moments of closeness with nature remind me of the privileged position I am in; hopefully I can do a good job and add my small input to the effort of conserving the island for the species we share it with.

At Bull Hole I met Maria doing her Guillemot population counts. One of the Common Buzzards from the nest up on the cliffs circled over the hide for a while, at times motionless with wings outspread on a current of air that allowed it to hover as still as a Kestrel and watch the scene below. Soon its chicks will be ready to fledge, as will those at the nest near the Amos. Fledglings are appearing across the island, from the tiny Wren in the vegetation by the washing lines as I hung up my clothes, to Curlew and Little Owl chicks seen today by Sarah and Maria.

14th: This morning I walked down to North Haven to meet Holly, Dave, Robin and three of the Oxford field trip party, Tara, Linda and Nicole, to help out with Kittiwake ringing at South Stream cliffs. It was a warm, sunny day, perfect for the job. To reach the cliffs from the research path we had to scramble over the black, slanting basalt of the foreshore, firstly climbing a few feet downwards with a rope as a failsafe. There we stopped, directly below the Sea Mayweed and lichen-covered rocks where the research path meets the shore. From here we watched Dave attempt to capture some of the adult birds nesting close to the foot of the cliff. At this point the cliff curves around to the south, with two shallow caves beneath its highest point, forming a sheltered, picturesque cove.

A hollow metal pole was used to capture the birds, containing a cord that forms a noose where it protrudes from the 'business end' of the implement. By pulling on a strap that emerges from the other end, the operator can tighten the noose. The pole was slowly raised by Dave to hover close to the chosen individual, and the noose gently edged towards and over its head. It was then tightened, and the bird plucked quickly from the ledge and swung out and down to be caught – in this case by Holly. Oddly, the Kittiwakes often showed only slight puzzlement at the appearance of the pole and the gentle draping of a noose around their heads, only starting up as the cord tightened. Probably the implement is sufficiently different from any stimulus they have evolved to respond to that they have no instinctive reaction to its presence. This is not to say that they never react; any movement by Dave could cause them to flush from the cliff, whilst others appear almost trapped, only to force themselves out of the noose at the last moment. Given the length of the pole and the uneven, slippery rocks on which the catcher had to stand, it is a skilful – and often frustrating – task, like a fairground ride with the odds stacked against you. It is worth noting that the Kittiwakes, whether captured or merely flushed from their nest, return quickly after circling the cliffs for a few seconds, regaining their usual behaviour apparently unperturbed by the experience. If a couple of attempts to catch any individual failed, Dave moved on to a new area.

The birds on the first area of cliff were too flighty to be caught, and we edged around this jutting section to the curving main face, picking our way over the barnacle-covered rocks beneath, with the clear sea to one side, the caves to the other; I was reminded of the bay where the Seals pupped in Ronald

Lockley's *Seal Woman*. Above us, the cliff-face (which I was used to viewing from the path as a vertical, two-dimensional surface) overhung in a series of rough galleries – parallel shelves following the grain of the rock from where the Kittiwakes peered down at us like spectators staring into a gladiator arena. The air was filled with birds, gently circling with the sunlight shining through their wings as they glided, showing each delicate detail of the feathers that combine to make such a powerful and efficient whole.

We stopped again, and here Dave was successful noosing several birds in quick succession. Once captured, they were either retrieved in mid-air as Dave swung the pole around, or he gently laid them onto a flat area of rock for a helper to pick up. I had a go myself; you hold the bird firmly enough to keep its wings folded in and with your other hand gently free the noose around its neck. The cord does not bite or choke the gull, which is protected by its snow-white plumage. Quickly a cloth bag is placed over the bird, which lies still once its head is inside, the bag shielding you from its sharp beak. The bird can breathe easily but cannot see its handlers, and there is an immediately calming effect. Close up Kittiwakes are handsome, with the upper feathers of their wings a smooth grey and their legs – the centre of attention for our task – reptilian and black.

There were two purposes of today's task. Firstly, birds that have not previously been ringed are each given a metal British Trust for Ornithology (BTO) ring, which is attached to the right leg. In addition, each Kittiwake receives a colour ring and a 'Darvik' ring. The latter carries a number that can be read from a distance without capturing the bird, while the unique arrangement of the colour rings (there may be up to three) forms a code for future identification. Each of the BTO rings has an individual number, so that if the bird is subsequently caught by any ringer, or found dead, it can be identified via the BTO database. This allows information on the movement of each bird to be built up, perhaps locally, perhaps across continents, depending on the species. Notes are made on the condition of the birds, and they are weighed and have the length of their wings measured, from the carpal (which would be the wrist in a human) to the end of the longest flight feather.

A Kittiwake about to be ringed

Over the years, the BTO ringing programme has created a huge store of information that can be used to research changes in the survival of birds and to understand the movement of each individual through its life. For example, the data can be used to see how the weight of migratory birds alters before, during and after their journey, to study the development of young birds or to spot trends in mortality. Ecological problems that cause birds to die can be traced to particular locations and causes. Sarah explained to me that ringing is probably the only way that this type of information can be gathered, especially for species too small to be fitted with GPS devices, which in any case could not be applied to anywhere near the same volume of birds.

As with every human endeavour, our frailties can undermine our efforts, however well intentioned we are. Some ringers can come to regard the act of ringing itself as the most important part of the process rather than a means to an important end, becoming caught up by the idea of ringing more birds faster. This type of compulsion can have consequences; birds ringed poorly may develop problems with their legs, and there can be a lack of attention to the disturbance caused by the ringing expedition itself. A system of licences and ringing supervisors minimises such issues, ensuring that high quality ringing work continues to improve our understanding of these fantastic species. Across the country the dedication and skill of hundreds of ringers provide much new knowledge about birds and their ecology.

The second reason for visiting the cliffs today was to recapture a number of birds with geolocators: tiny electronic chips that are attached to a leg ring and collect information on the movement of the bird for up to two years. The locator can be plugged into a laptop or hand-held device for the information to be downloaded, providing a wealth of data for the researchers to examine. Today Holly was collecting and replacing locators as and when we caught birds carrying them. As the birds return to the same nest site each year they can be found easily, although catching them is a different matter.

By about half past twelve we called it a day; the remaining birds had become alert to our presence, and it was not worth continuing to disturb them. As we left we found a Sea Gooseberry in a tiny rock pool beneath the cliffs. These transparent creatures are (as their name suggests) gooseberry-shaped, with 'rungs' of miniscule horizontal ridges arranged into columns and spreading downwards from one tip to the other, each ridge depressing in quick succession and causing waves of movement to course over its body like an electric current. It lay completely still in its cereal bowl-sized world of seawater, only the rhythmic pulses of its jelly-like surface betraying life.

The afternoon was spent in the routine round of Guillemot surveying. At the Wick the evening light picked out the birds well, and I found new chicks at 1 and 2G. Later, researchers from the Oxford field trip were heading out to Tom's House to trap and ring Storm Petrels, and I got the chance to go along and observe. The Storm Petrels nest among the boulders and scree beneath the overhanging cliff-face to the south of the inlet, bounded to the north by a steep slope of Yorkshire Fog, Sea Mayweed and Marsh Pennywort where water trickles through the vegetation towards the sea. They are caught in mist nets, hung between poles about seven feet tall across the bottom of the boulder field. The nets are divided into compartments so that, when the birds hit, the section of net bulges and closes behind them, and they fall into a kind of pouch where they are trapped without getting too tangled in the lines. Tim and another researcher waited by the nets to collect the birds, while Tara, Ben and I sat higher up on the grassy slope.

It was a blustery night with flurries of drizzle that luckily lessened as we settled to wait. The sky still held some light although it was well after ten, and we could make out the promontory of jagged rocks that jutted out west from the Amos, a black silhouette against the navy and grey sky and the dark waves flecked with white. As we talked, the Irish ferry came into view, a light studded wedge ploughing south to Pembroke. In the night, the warm glow from its portholes and the thrum of its engines were reassuring; from the cold, dark prehistoric landscape we watched a fragment of modern life passing across the empty sea, occupants asleep or in the bar, readying themselves for the next part of their journey. Then it was gone, and we were again alone with the wind and the rocks and the shouting Oystercatchers.

At about eleven, with moonlight shining through the ragged clouds over the shoulder of the Amos, we moved down the slope. Tim and Ella brought the first two Storm Petrels down from the net inside soft cloth bags. Seeing them close-up, their nomadic lifestyle spent roaming the oceans, seems unbelievable. They are small, perhaps sparrow-size, and except for a white rump and some white feathers under their wings are completely black. Looking at the underside of the bird, the white feathers of the rump appear to meet the black tail feathers in a clean line, but on closer inspection their tips are also black, as if someone had gone over the edges when they were being painted. The birds seem delicate, with forewings measuring only around 12cm and tiny black triangular feet with which they patter over the waves to collect the offal and fragments of sea-life that they eat (the Latin name of their genus – *Hydrobates* – means 'water walker'). Their feathers are soft and shiny, and carry a sweet musty smell like camphor oil, a signal that plays a part in attracting mates. Like related birds, such as the Fulmar and the Shearwater, Storm Petrels have nasal tubules at the top of their beaks allowing them to filter salt from the seawater and so survive without fresh water.

Each bird caught was weighed (most were only around 80g) and given a metal BTO ring before being released. I was able to let one go; it sat still and light for a moment on my hand before fluttering into the dark, falling onto the soft grass and then finally disappearing to circle the rocks above us. The researchers caught about 12 birds before the winds grew stronger and we finished for the night.

Back on the plateau I saw Glow-worms for the first time, their green lights like LEDs placed amidst the vegetation. The abdominal segments of the females shine to attract mates, the glow caused by an enzyme – luciferase – acting on the energy producing molecule ATP (Adenosine Triphosphate) within their bodies. The points of light were scattered in the Bracken all along the path back to the farm, still, silent and somehow calming in their constancy and gentle colour.

15th: This morning I had the chance to join Dave, Holly, Maria and Phil (one of the Shearwater researchers) as they went out to ring Razorbill chicks and collect geolocators from adult birds at the Basin. To reach the nest sites, we half walked, half slid down the steep slope at Tom's House, past the place where the mist nets had been set for the Storm Petrels the night before, scrambling over the wet boulders of the foreshore and up to the natural archway that forms the entrance to the Basin. Looking through the basalt frame to the teeming Guillemot colony on the Amos was like looking through a portal to some lost world, the birds lining the ancient rocks seeming not too distant from their reptilian ancestors.

We walked beneath the arch, the base and walls covered in smooth, rounded lumps of rock, where the molten stone had bubbled and set during its volcanic birth. Dropping down amid the boulders on the other side, the arm of the Amos curved around us, open towards Skokholm, grey and indistinct in the drizzle. This was the shore I had previously contemplated from the hide above, not thinking I would be able to view it from ground level. As we clambered round to the gully where the Razorbills nest, the sea seemed almost to be higher than the boulders we edged between, and we had to time our movements to avoid being drenched by the crashing breakers.

The gully we arrived in lies between the Amos hide and the shoulder of that rocky promontory. To the left and right above us on the scree slope were some of the Fulmar colonies I had surveyed from the cliff-tops. Dave began searching for Razorbills, which were hooked by the feet with a length of wire and pulled from their nest sites deep in crevices between the jumbled boulders. These birds can give a nasty bite and even in a cloth bag require careful handling. The chicks are similar to those of the Guillemots, dark grey and downy with soft-looking wings like those of a cuddly toy, and beaks less bold and heavy than those of their parents. Their shouts can be piercing as they wait indignantly to be ringed, weighed and have their wings measured. We found a variety of ages of chick, some still fairly small and others close to fledging (when, like the Guillemot chicks, they will make their way to the sea to be taught to dive and feed by their fathers). Several chicks were ringed, and a couple of geolocators retrieved for downloading and analysis before we stopped for chocolate and squash, sitting on the rocks and looking out over the sea, with the black, white and grey mosaic of the Amos in the foreground.

The day offered a final experience when the volunteers called us outside after dinner to the see the end of a lunar eclipse. By the time we rounded the end of the farm buildings the moon was full and low in the southern sky above the ridge, its right-hand third darkened by the crescent shadow of the Earth. Through Sarah's 'scope each crater and scar on its pale surface was visible, the distance between me and that ancient satellite somehow accentuated by the detail, observed with the knowledge that each minute line or pattern was in reality likely to be many miles long.

After the eclipse I climbed up to the trig point, the dark island stretching away on all sides, the sea towards St Ann's Head reflecting the silver moonlight. Skokholm was a silhouette, without detail apart from the white and red-shaded flash of its lighthouse, answered by the blinking lights from St Ann's Head and The Smalls. Across the sickle-shaped bay the South Bishop light joined its sisters, glinting like a diamond beyond the floodlit tankers, at the tip of the rugged chain of land; St David's peninsular, Ramsey, the Bishops and Clerks isles. Once more the ferry was following its slow, inevitable course between Skomer and Grassholm, guided by those lights. I felt, perhaps for the first time this summer, my own position; on the western tip of Wales, beyond it even, with rock-broken heath and the crying birds all around me, a landscape marked under my gaze by pinpricks of light, the open sea and the moon a beautiful, aching reminder of a longer timeframe, a scale larger than our lives, packed with experience and detail that our thoughts cannot encompass or imagine. This scene, dark, cold in the night breeze, filled me with an enthusiasm, a lifting of my spirits beyond daily concerns, in a way that no sunlit vista could; its power is the contrast between the timeless, endless span of nature and our own fleeting lives, the comfort and opportunity that comes from being a part of that scene.

16th: Today Maria, Sarah, her friend Sam and I took a trip to the mainland for a pub lunch and a few drinks. After examining Sue's OS map I also had some archaeological exploration to do: Above North Haven, and silhouetted against the skyline as you approach the island by boat, is the Harold Stone. Believed to date from the Iron Age or earlier, its purpose remains unclear. Theories about the stone range from it being used as a signal to anyone approaching the island by sea, to that it was used as a cattle rubbing stone, or that it had an undefined ceremonial significance. What was interesting to me was the fact that just north of Broad Haven on the mainland is a village called Haroldston, close to which is marked a standing stone, labelled 'Harold Stone'. Looking at the map it appears that the mainland and Skomer Harold Stones should be visible to each other across St Bride's Bay. Could the two stones be associated? Taken together do they form a line towards a point of interest, say in the Preselis? It was certainly worth investigating, and, as the others planned to visit the shops before heading for lunch in Little Haven, I decided to disappear for an hour and find the mainland Harold Stone.

It was a sunny day as we crossed to the mainland, but a strong breeze cooled us as the *Dale Princess* took us over to Martin's Haven where we caught the 'Puffin Shuttle'[5] to Broad Haven. The bus sped past cottages, trees and hedges, fields of potatoes, meadows of wild flowers, meandering estuarine

---

[5] The 'Puffin Shuttle' is the local bus service, connecting the villages along the Pembrokeshire coast and allowing walkers to explore sections of the coast path without driving.

streams that snaked to the sea amid beds of reeds, tiny villages, walls covered with Red Valerian, banks of Foxglove, Red Campion and Sheep's Bit Scabious. The countryside poured by, a flow of memory-stirring summer scenes, tableaus of rural life on a rapidly warming June morning. Everything seemed rich with colour: flowers, hedgerows, painted cottage walls, heat radiating from short, browning lawns, the cool of spreading beech trees. I made no attempt to think, just watched it pass, until we had wound our way to the sea front at Broad Haven. Here we left the bus, and I set off to search for the Harold Stone.

The path from the sea meandered out of town alongside a small stream, climbing gently and lined with willow and thick, verdant scrub that merged into woodland. The air was humid and heavy with the smell of vegetation, the route freshly cleared by brush cutters, carving a path through the undergrowth, the cavern of the trees echoing with birdsong. After the bare, open landscape of the island I felt immersed in nature; scents, sounds, colours filled my senses as I made my way upwards. The path brought me to the tiny church of St Madoc of Ferns. According to a leaflet in the church porch, St Madoc is a derivation of St Aiden, who probably founded the isolated chapel as a place of quiet meditation. I sat for a while in the cool, grey stone church and enjoyed the peaceful atmosphere.

Moving on I walked along a narrow, winding lane until I found the field where the Harold Stone was marked, scattered with Creeping Buttercups and Common Mouse-ear and overlooking St Bride's Bay. The stone itself was less impressive than its island counterpart; a large boulder in the centre of the field, but looking out over the bay I saw that Skomer was indeed visible from the spot. Not a marker for the Preselis though; there was no view inland, but the direction of Skomer suggested to me a possible alignment with the setting sun, perhaps at the winter solstice. An interpretation board at Broad Haven had informed me that an Iron Age fort had been sited close to the stone along the coast, linking this landscape to the settlements on Skomer from the same era of pre-history. Deciding to research the two stones further when I returned to the island, I headed along the coast path to join the others at The Swan in Little Haven.

There was a fresh wind blowing off the sea as I walked bare-footed along the sandy beach between Broad Haven and Little Haven. The sunny weather was retreating against a curtain of rain moving in from the west, spectacular and somehow exhilarating, bringing me close to the elements in the cold spray of the shower. I was eventually glad to reach Little Haven and join the others for a pub meal and a couple of pints. We had a relaxing afternoon sitting in the terrace beer garden and watching life pass by on the sea front: a horse-rider setting out along the beach, a fisherman preparing his gear, builders at work on sea-wall restoration and on the Red Valerian flowers Scarlet Tiger moths being hunted by a sharp-eyed Jackdaw. The afternoon slipped away pleasantly until it was time to take a taxi ride back to Martin's Haven and the boat home.

In the evening Chris cooked us all tea up at the farm, and after Bird Log at North Haven we stayed and chatted, flicking through the various field guides and journals in the library and enjoying a couple of cans of Ruddles County before returning to the farm, tired but relaxed.

17th: Friday dawned wet and misty, with gales from the sea allowing me to lie in slightly longer than usual before taking the chance to get my data input up to date. At lunchtime I walked down to the Bull Hole hide and, by the early evening, conditions had improved enough for me to survey at the Wick, although it was a cold and damp experience. The volunteers provided a meal in the old farm later, and there were the usual drinks in the old warden's cabin, although I turned in early, tired from the experiences of the week.

18th: After a morning at Bull Hole I came back to the farm to meet Amelia, who was down in Pembroke for the weekend with Danny; unfortunately he was not well enough to come over, but it was good to see Amelia and catch up with the news from Aberystwyth. We had a good walk around the island, and despite the wind I managed to set the 'scope up so she could see one of the growing number of large Guillemot chicks on the cliff-face at the Wick. As always with these visits, it seemed only a short while before it was time for the afternoon boat, but it was an enjoyable day, and I like passing on my experiences and knowledge of the island.

After an evening of survey work at the Wick I was glad to spend a quiet evening watching an action film on TV and writing up my journal: a pause in the rich deluge of experience that island life brings, despite its isolation from the hectic mainland world. It is difficult to work out exactly why life is so full here despite the cutting off of so much everyday complexity. I suppose it has something to do with the ever-changing weather from the sea, the face of which is never still and never the same, the cycle of the breeding seasons of the seabirds, owls, curlews, pipits, water fowl; the growing, flowering, wilting, entwining of the vegetation. This change is seemingly suppressed in the static and inflexible landscape of houses, roads and shops, the apparent stable constancy of technology. In such a world we can imagine things still and permanent. Here the seasons press on, the first signs of the next part of a cycle always visible even as the previous part is at its climax. There can be a sense of urgency, of headlong, teeming life, interacting, competing, never still, night as diverse and full as day. One has to pull away from these details and view the landscape in its vastness, at the level of its rocky skeleton, the wide sky and sweep of sea, in order to find calmness and peace, to be content with the idea of constant change, not to be so swept up in it that peace is lost in the confusion of an endless cycling race.

Guillemot with chick

19<sup>th</sup>: The round of Guillemot sites is becoming easier as each chick grows, and those belonging to birds obscured at the back of ledges are now large enough to be seen as they bob up and down in front of their parent or tentatively explore the ledge, occasionally pausing to flap their tiny black wings. Downy feathers are slowly replaced by smooth adult plumage, except on the head, which retains a woolly appearance even as the pattern of white and black around the eyes develops. The older chicks have white above the eye and under the chin, making them look more like penguins than Guillemots, their bills still relatively small. The only surveying issue arises when wandering birds nestle up to different adults. This can lead to some second guessing of previous recordings until the chick finally totters back to its parent, burrowing into the thick feathers under its wing (when they are larger this position of comfort leaves their head protruding behind the adult, their tail sticking out at the front). It is a positive feeling to know that each growing chick is approaching fledging, some already old enough (16 days) to count as successfully fledged; my task is entering its final stage. Apart from the survey work, it has been a quiet day on the island, routine after the experiences of the previous week.

20<sup>th</sup>: Aware that tomorrow is the longest day, my thoughts have turned back to the Harold Stone and the position of the sun relative to a line between it and its mainland namesake. I visited the stone, confirming that the headland north of Broad Haven is visible from there. I also found a website that calculates the position of the setting sun on different dates and at different times. With this information I can see how the stone's position relates to sunrise and sunset at the solstice and equinox[6].

Harold Stone and St Bride's Bay

I was able to survey Bull Hole but little else; a fairly bright morning became cold and misty, and by the time I attempted the Wick conditions had worsened; I received a soaking and could do no work. I took refuge in the researchers' kitchen, drinking tea and doing crosswords, while the sea and the rest of

[6] In 2012, I visited the Harold Stone at sunrise on the summer solstice. From the stone, the mid-summer sun breaks the horizon in the centre of a cleft in the nearby rocky outcrop; a striking finding that suggests the stone was deliberately placed to produce such an alignment. It is unclear whether the Preselis, lying beyond the outcrop on the horizon, had any relevance to this relationship between the stone and the solstice sun. The Royal Commission on the Ancient and Historical Monuments of Wales (details at the back of the book) are planning to undertake more research on the stone.

the island disappeared into the fog. I joined Jess, Sue, Maria and Kate for tea. Kate is visiting from Skokholm where she is the long-term volunteer; Sarah has swapped with her to learn the island routines so she can cover when Jerry is away. We had a lovely meal of halloumi in tomato sauce with pasta and salad, then, after we had worked for a while on the obligatory after-dinner crossword puzzles, I turned in for the evening, hoping for a drier day tomorrow!

21st: I put in a long morning of surveying, beginning at Wick Corner and then moving down to South Stream cliffs to complete the Kittiwake plots. It was high tide and the azure sea smacked and crashed hollowly into the caves under the cliff-face. I found Bog Pimpernel in flower by the stand of Square-stalked St John's-wort, where the tumbling vegetation of the slope meets the basalt of the foreshore. The trailing stems are adorned with delicate blooms, white petals broken up by thin lines of pink-purple. I saw a number of Kittiwake chicks before moving round the island to spend the afternoon at Bull Hole.

On the north coast path, Self-heal is in flower and clumps of tiny cream-white Heath Bedstraw flowers frost the vegetation of the Skomer Head Rabbit exclosure. I finished the day surveying the third Kittiwake plot at the Wick and at Moory Mere hide saw a stand of Skullcap in flower by the path. A new succession of species is coming into bloom after the June gap in floral resources (which bees often struggle through) between the flowers of spring and those of high and late summer. The new flowers bring new colours, including the various purples of the Marsh, Creeping and Spear Thistles that line the island pathways. Most of the bees I have seen appear to be the Common Carder-bee (*Bombus pascuorum*), but it would be interesting to catch a few, as the rarer Brown-banded Carder-bee (*B. humilis*) and Large Carder-bee (*B. muscorum*) look similar and may also be on the island. After a full day I was grateful to have dinner with Sue, Jess, Maria and Kate; we have been lucky enough to be given the leftovers from the Cardiff group's catering (they brought a chef with them to the island!); this evening chilli and a glass of red wine.

22nd: Today I set myself the ambitious target of surveying all the Wick sites for Guillemots, as well as the Kittiwake sites on the cliff, in preparation for taking the weekend off for a trip back to Aberystwyth. Luckily the weather was kind and I got most of the Wick completed in the morning. After lunch Kate joined me to survey Bull Hole and to help with the Kittiwakes at the Wick. She was impressed by the fact that, as a result of surveying the site for so many hours, I was able to scan the Guillemots at Bull Hole and call out around 200 territory numbers from memory as she wrote down their status. I am not sure if this 'skill' is a matter for pride or concern! We were able to finish the remaining sites by about seven and return for a well-earned tea: delicious tuna fish cakes made by Sue, a glass of white wine and a feeling of satisfaction at getting through my work.

23rd: By half past ten I had completed the Bull Hole survey. It was a calm day, the sea and sky still and grey as I walked down to catch the twelve o'clock boat. At the steps someone had spotted that a pair of Razorbills occupying a crevice close to the path had a chick, and there were three or more Guillemot chicks on the small ledge below. After spending so much time watching the birds through the 'scope, it was good to see them so close, with the Puffins splashing in the waters of North Haven below. It was interesting to see how small the Guillemots are in 'real life'; magnified by the lens of the 'scope, I had come to think of them as quite large, there being few scale references on the cliff-faces. And then I was aboard the *Dale Princess*, looking forward to a weekend in Aberystwyth.

27th: I returned to the island yesterday, and a visit to the Wick revealed that a number of Guillemots have already left, with still more gone today. In the morning, however, I was able to turn my attention away from Guillemots as Dave had invited us in groups of two or three to join him in capturing and ringing Puffin chicks on the isthmus (as if to emphasize their attractiveness, these chicks are referred to as pufflings). Sue and I took the morning shift.

The idea is to use lengths of wire with a blunted hook at one end to feel for (and if possible pull out) any chick or adult in the burrow. This involves lying flat on the ground with your arm up to the shoulder in the burrow, first exploring the entrance with your hand, then using the wire to delve deeper. There is some risk of getting a sharp bite from an adult bird, or even a Shearwater, so these first explorations carry some nervous excitement (I was reminded of the character in Flash Gordon, putting his hand into different holes in a tree trunk as part of a Russian roulette-style initiation test, with a deadly stinging reptile hiding in one). The job is not for the squeamish either, feeling around in bird droppings and mud, with the burrows teeming with ticks. It is hard to tell if any lump or unusual shape within a burrow is a chick or just an area of softer soil. Only when you feel (somewhat startlingly) a movement against the wire can you be sure you have found a bird, although a good sign is finding traces of down on the hook when it is gently withdrawn. Once found, it is even more difficult to work out the size of the chick, how it is sitting and whether you are moving to catch it too hesitantly, dangerously fast or in completely the wrong direction! Although both Sue and I located a couple of chicks each, we ended up calling Dave over to get the birds out.

The chicks are fairly large now, some with wings free of down and with a shadow of their eye pattern and facemask marked in their feathers. Their beaks are still dark, thinner than the wide colourful ones of the adults, the inside of the mouth a pale colour like white chocolate and likewise the soft elastic skin at the hinge of the beak; this may be a mechanism to hold onto fish or help seal the mouth when the bird dives. The slit in the facial feathers of the adults, running back from the eye (similar to that in Guillemots), is also of ambiguous use but may act to take sea water away from the eyes during diving.

Young Puffin

Pufflings reach a maximum weight of about 350g before fledging, losing some of this weight before they leave, and their forewings grow to about 13cm. Dave explained that, towards the end of the six weeks it takes for them to fledge, large chicks emerge from their burrows at dusk to flap their wings in preparation for taking to the air. My ringing attempts were somewhat clumsy, and I found that a particular type of strength in the fingers and thumb is required to push the metal ring together around the leg before the pliers are used – a strength that I apparently lack! There is also a skill in pressing the ends of the ring together with the pliers so that they do not overlap, ensuring that they sit with their edges joined smoothly without a step (either problem could cause the leg to graze and callous over time). I managed to ring one bird – with a fair bit of assistance – and wished it a successful life.

After a cup of tea at North Haven and lunch at the farm, I was able to get around my Guillemot sites by early evening; the fact that chicks are now leaving the nest provides a definite end-of-season feel to the colonies, with gaps appearing in usually packed areas and non-breeding birds taking up unfamiliar positions on the rocks. It is hard to avoid feeling that the birds with late chicks must be concerned or feel left behind as the structure of the colony dissolves around them, but of course they continue as normal; the concerns are my own. After dinner Sue and I walked down to High Cliff to watch the fledglings jumping. Each chick is persuaded by its mother to launch itself from the ledge, tumbling down the cliff-face to the sea or rocks below. Somehow they survive these jolting falls intact, cushioned by thick feathers, their undersized wings at least slowing their precipitous descent. We watched from close to the shoreline, High Cliff towering over us against a darkening summer sky, and we could hear the high-pitched cheeps of the chicks in the colony. Below, rafts of males called up to their young, the scene regarded balefully by 'Greaters' on the boulders under the cliff.

For half an hour or so little happened; a pair of Fulmars gurgled at each other in the mouth of the hollow they occupied close by us on the grassy slope, Puffins, Razorbills, Guillemots and Kittiwakes flew to and fro, the sea ebbed and flowed, and the aspect of the cliff-face changed in the dying light. Then suddenly there was a splash, a flurry of activity among the adult birds on the water. Our first fledgling was in fact a Razorbill chick, its parent racing to its side before both swam quickly away over the silver-edged water to the safety of the open sea. Then we saw a couple of Guillemot chicks successfully claimed by their parent, before a fourth lingered too long on the boulders and was taken and carried away, still struggling, by a 'Greater'. Later another was pulled from the sea by one of these large, intimidating predators, dead before its parent could reach it. A second of indecision or a poorly timed jump was all it took to destroy the fruit of months of effort undertaken by each pair of Guillemots; but it was not a waste to the 'Greater' chicks waiting on the rocky crags for their next meal. After watching a couple more successful leapers, we scrambled back up the slope to the path. The final part of the Guillemot journey from conception to fledging was underway, and I had viewed it from start to finish, a snapshot of the continuing cycle that brought me some affinity with the species, their lives and their daily experience of colony life.

Gull Chicks

28th: Today I made my first return visit to the 25 'Greater' nests that Chris and I had located and checked for eggs back in May. Last year the checks for large young were done in the second week of July, but already the chicks were large and mobile, and I decided to get in a visit a little earlier. The surveying handbook advised me to attempt to count the chicks from a distance before approaching each nest; when alarmed, they scurry from the rocks into the Bracken where their patterning provides good camouflage in the dry summer vegetation. As they totter, head down, into the undergrowth they resemble elderly men, hunched over and carrying heavy shopping, or against the skyline like pre-historic reptiles, showing vestiges of their ancient lineage.

At first I had some success in spotting and counting chicks, but on the longer ridges the nest sites and chicks were often obscured from a distance; as I got close enough to see, the adults rose heavily into the warm afternoon air, and their young escaped unseen. Their camouflage is highly effective; at one point I startled one hiding close to a rock within touching distance. As I moved onto the nests that Chris had surveyed, things were more difficult still as I did not have my own memory of the nest sites to work from. Eventually, hot and tired, I returned to the farm and from there Jess and I went down to North Haven for a swim. We were closely observed by two inquisitive Grey Seals who watched our progress with shining brown eyes before ducking below the waves in a swirl of water, while Puffins and Razorbills floated lazily on the calm water.

29th: My friends Deborah and Ian and their daughter Hetty had driven over from their camping holiday in Tenby to visit, but a mix up meant that they missed the morning boat, and instead I took the *Dale Princess* to Martin's Haven to join them on the mainland, having completed surveying my (now sparsely populated) Guillemot sites in the morning. We had a pleasant lunch at the St Bride's Inn in Little Haven, sitting in the beer garden and catching up with our news.

It seems a long time since I have been home to Macclesfield, and it was good to see them all. After an afternoon on the beach, I headed back in time for the afternoon boat. On the way over to the island Kenny spotted two Gannets fighting over a large Garfish. These are slender fish and this one was at least 15cm long, shining silver in the afternoon sun. Despite the size of its prize, the victor of the struggle simply tipped its head back and swallowed the fish whole, and we left the sleek, huge bird bobbing on the waves as we neared Skomer.

Crossing the channel perhaps ten times a day, the boatmen know the wildlife of the area as well as anyone. While I watch the birds on land, they see them in the marine environment to which they are best adapted. Through their work, Kenny and Carl have a connection with St Bride's Bay– with the natural landscape – that so many have lost, as jobs have become further and further removed from the land, and the sea.

In the evening there was a shared meal in the old farm to mark the end of Maria's stay as the long-term volunteer. She displayed the impressive identification boards she had painted for the public hides, and Ben brought out one of his speciality cakes, this one shaped and decorated like a Shearwater chick waiting to be ringed!

30th: I slept poorly last night – it was warm and muggy – and drifted restlessly until at least three or four; I was bleary eyed and grateful for a bacon sandwich made by Sue on my way out to survey the Wick sites. There are only three or four chicks left at 1G, maybe a dozen at Wick Corner. By half eleven all of us had gathered at the landing steps to see Maria off; there were final photos in the sunshine and then she was gone, the *Dale Princess* cutting across the shining waters towards the mainland.

The end of season feeling intensified for me, with the first of our team disappearing. Up until now life on the island has been about arrivals – of eggs, of chicks, of people – now the theme is one of departure and ending. Despite the high summer sun and azure skies, the days themselves are shortening again, and the need to plan for the future percolates my thoughts. I joined Dave, Ben and Annette for some tea at North Haven before wandering up North Valley with Dave in search of butterflies. I last followed this path when the 'Lessers' were nurturing their warm mottled eggs on nests dotting the tumbledown walls and areas of low vegetation. Now the Bracken and Marsh Thistles are high, swathes of Water Pepper mark wetter areas and stands of Purple Loosestrife were beginning to burst into flower.

The gulls filled the sky around us as we approached, but there was no real mobbing, and we failed to see any chicks in the main nesting area. Dave suspected it would be a poor breeding season for the 'Lessers'; their numbers are in decline, possibly because over the last thirty years the size of the fishing fleet and accompanying edible waste has decreased massively. There is an argument that the populations will just fall back to their 'natural' level, but, given that the state of the oceans is far from natural, this remains to be seen. The term 'natural level' itself suggests a risk-free stability that the constant variation of the natural world could never produce; life is about change, cycles, shocks and risk.

We saw a few Common Blue damselflies, dark, chocolate-brown Ringlets fluttering among the Bracken fronds, Meadow

Browns sharing the thistle heads with countless bumblebees – small, pale *B. pascuorum* workers enjoying the nectar of the purple inflorescences, and a Large Skipper at rest amidst the Bracken close to the North Pond research hide. Apparently, the upper reaches of North Valley above Green Pond and the corridor of vegetation along the low wall up towards North Pond are good areas to see Dark Green Fritillaries, although there were none in evidence today.

It was half past three by the time I returned to the farm for a late lunch before walking up to Bull Hole to check the few remaining birds with chicks and to reflect, as the ferry ploughed through the waves on the horizon, that there may be very few more times that its progress will punctuate an afternoon of Guillemot observation.

# *July*

Kittiwake with chick

1<sup>st</sup>: I spent the morning searching the rocky outcrops of North Wick ridge for 'Greater' chicks with Chris, finding vantage points from which to view the open, slanting hill tops under a hot sun. We had some success and a good tour of the south of the island; despite the recent rain, South Pond is dry, a bed of rusty-flowered Common Sorrel, with the 'Lessers' scattered amongst the vegetation watching over their young.

After lunch I continued surveying the northern part of the island alone. Scanning Marble Rocks for chicks, it was striking to see the crag and Bracken-covered country set against the backdrop of super-tankers shimmering in the afternoon heat, the northern peninsular of St David's forming a crooked line behind them. With most of the island covered, I met Jess at North Haven for a refreshing swim; the water seemed a little warmer, though not quite Mediterranean yet! Around eight, I wandered up to the Garland Stone before Bird Log, meeting Sarah in North Valley. She pointed out a couple of Linnets perched in a clump of Brambles; red-breasted finches that chatter to each other as they fly in exuberant flocks across the island; she said they reminded her of small Kestrels in their colouring. Although I found no porpoises at the Garland Stone, I enjoyed watching the Gannets circling low over the waves. In the distance the *Dale Princess* was out on the bay close to a tanker (she is sometimes employed taking supplies to the ships), dwarfed by its massive hull. The contrast in size reminded me just how huge these now-familiar ships are, how big the business of oil production and transport is, how, beside it, our own lives are as tiny as the *Dale Princess* out on the sea under the bows of the tankers.

2nd: With only a handful of Guillemots remaining, I had completed a full survey of sites by lunchtime despite the sweltering heat of the island under a blue-white sky. The afternoon was spent analysing data, the early evening drinking wine in the farm garden with Jess, Sue and two of Sue's friends visiting from the Netherlands. The time drifted pleasantly as we talked, and later Sue cooked Sea Bass and Red Snapper with dill and roast vegetables for tea, summery and welcome to the wine-softened palate. It was good to talk to Sue's friends; one was interested in the use of herbs in healing, and both shared my belief in the importance of the whole over the parts in nature and in ourselves. Our conversation was heartening, making me feel my attempts to develop and share my own ideas was important enough to continue, and that I could perhaps find people open enough to receive a new perspective and maybe even change things slightly for the better.

After tea we rushed through North Valley to the coast to try to catch the sunset, arriving at the crest of the ridge in time to see the sun slide into a silver-blue ocean beyond South Bishop lighthouse, disappearing with a twinkle of green and leaving the dome of sky a faded peach, blue-grey in the darkening east, the sea like silk divided only by the low silhouette of a tanker slipping in front of Grassholm. As the light grew softer, we scrambled down to Payne's Ledge, a hidden Guillemot colony occupying a single horizontal crevice low on the cliffs. We sat on the spongy, Rabbit-cropped grass and listened to the gargling calls of the birds and the shrill cheeping of their chicks, but none of the few remaining youngsters jumped. Just below us a couple of downy-grey Herring Gull chicks wandered on the rocks around their nest; the coming night was signalled by the flashing of the Smalls Lighthouse. At the end of the dark peninsular of St David's, rising and falling above the sheen of sea like a serpent, came the reply of the light at South Bishop. We headed back to the farm with the cool night air on the Bracken, sweet with the scent of vegetation and earth.

3$^{rd}$-8$^{th}$: This week has marked the end of the Guillemot season, barring a few late fledgers, and an end to the island routine that had, unnoticed, become important to me. Two events marked the change; Jess left on Tuesday and the new long-term volunteer, James, arrived on the island. As always I found the change difficult; living in a small community, every person plays a part in each day, in every aspect of life. Subconsciously we mould around each other, forming bonds that are only recognised as they are broken, leaving one with a sense of emptiness, and sometimes regret at not making more of a period of time that, apparently slow in its experience, is passed in an instant. The feelings that were drawn out across that time are condensed in retrospect to an intense melancholy that, if it had been expected, could have been eased by a word or action at the right time. Characteristically I take a somewhat melodramatic view of the change!

Work, of course, continues and I have embarked on the fourth round of Kittiwake surveying. Many birds have large chicks now; their wings lose the downy white-grey fluff of the first days after hatching, gain black tips, grey adult plumage, and lengthen. When they exceed the length of the tail by 1-2cm the chicks are classed as fledged. By the time I return from my visit to Aberystwyth for my Ph.D. graduation, a fair few will have reached that stage, although in some other nests there are still white, downy young less than ten days old. In places, particularly at the Wick, nests present on earlier visits low on the cliff-face have vanished, victims of stormy waves crashing along the rocks at high tide. In other places there are groups of two or three abandoned nests clustered together, perhaps due to failed eggs or predation.

In addition to my Kittiwake round, I have continued to scan North Wick Ridge, South Plateau and Marble Rocks for 'Greater' chicks, trying to find vantage points from which I can spot the chicks without my presence driving them into the Bracken. So far I have seen 31 (from 67 eggs counted), but there are at least two sites I would like to revisit where I am certain there are chicks, if only I could find the right angle of approach.

Over the weekend the days were hot and still, allowing several swimming trips. Jess, Chris and I swam as far as the Loaf, a kelp-covered outcrop emerging from the waters of North Haven, onto which we clambered, breathless and ungainly, feeling the warmth of the rock and enjoying the bay from a new position. From Tuesday the weather itself changed, the sun left us and rain swept over the island in squalls on the northerly wind. It has, to some extent, suited my mood and at the same time allowed me some space from the field work to input data and begin to compile my results.

I attended Bird Log most evenings; tonight one of the volunteers – Charlie – had impressive pictures of an Ocean Sunfish he had seen off the Garland Stone during the day. The routine of the log, followed by episodes of *Dexter* watched with Dave, Chris, and Annette, has been good for me. The late viewing on Wednesday and Thursday meant I walked up from North Haven as the Shearwaters were flying in; a surreal experience.

On both nights it was raining hard. With my waterproof zipped right up, my head torch illuminated only a foot ahead of me, the light glinting off the shards of rain, and the pitch-dark country spreading away from that pool of light on all sides, filled with a cacophony of the throaty, cooing calls of the Shearwaters. Into the glow of my torch the birds would appear, lying or crawling on the track, fluttering away or freezing in the beam, their soft, dark backs beaded with drops of rain, unhurried by the ferocious wind that drove me on. I was tempted, for a moment, to feel that they too must be worried by the conditions, but of course they are not. A Skomer storm must be nothing compared to those they face out on the Atlantic as they skim the walls of dark water on their long migration to South America. Their presence, filling the night with noise and activity, is a comforting one, and I felt the privilege of passing through their strange nocturnal world, of experiencing the night and the island along with them.

9th: This morning I completed the latest set of Kittiwake counts before following the path from the Wick along the coast to check the 'Greater' sites along Marble Rocks. The high-pitched, slightly hoarse cheeps of 'Lesser' and 'Greater' chicks is an almost constant sound on any walk around the island now; their chequered brown forms stalk the skylines, crash through the Bracken or sometimes lie sleeping in the sunshine, with attentive adults always close.

The Bracken is higher now, Red Campion flowers scattered amongst it, no longer an unbroken carpet of pink. The sunny yellow flower heads of Ragwort are appearing, bursting open in dense clusters in the sunshine. Over the past few weeks the plants have grown tall, heavy foliage spreading from tough stalks, so that in some places the stands of this poisonous plant resemble copses of trees in lush summer foliage, dotting a parkland landscape like the pasture woodland of the New Forest in miniature. The effect is striking where the coast path leads uphill from the Amos research path to the north, where from a distance the herbs resemble the rounded, sturdy form of Horse-chestnut trees. Now the yellow blooms betray the illusion and provide a source of food for the insects, while the tiger-striped Cinnabar moth caterpillars are emerging to eat the foliage; in doing so they imbibe the toxins that protect them from would-be predators. A few red and black adult moths are flying too, the name 'Cinnabar' coming from that of the red pigment which their warning colouration resembles.

My third visit to Marble Rocks gave me a sight of three more chicks and completed my survey of the 'Greaters', so that I was free to go down to North Haven and help Annette to weigh the Shearwater chicks. The single egg of each Shearwater pair is incubated in the burrow for around 40 days, warmed by both adults in turn, and over the past couple of weeks these have begun to hatch. When the chick emerges, grey and thick with down, an adult usually remains with it for three or four days after which both parents leave the burrow to collect food. Three or four times a week, unless a bright full moon deters them, the adults return to feed their offspring regurgitated fish; the birds we were weighing already had full, rounded bellies under their down.

All the burrows in the survey are numbered and many have replaceable 'plugs' to allow access to the nest chamber: cones of wire mesh filled with earth and turf that can be removed when the birds need to be checked. The weighing routine is straightforward; kneeling or lying by the burrow, you put your arm inside, feeling gently for a chick whose down is so soft you can sometimes pass over them without noticing. Once found, the chick is removed carefully and placed in a yoghurt tub on a set of scales for weighing. They sit comically in the tub, with their tiny wings protruding over the sides looking around them, the youngest encountering daylight for the first time. Quickly they are returned to their burrow and replaced in the same position as they were found.

The smallest chicks we weighed were about 40g, the older two-week chicks well over 100g. When they eventually fledge they will be heavier than adult birds, weighing 480-550g, compared to an adult weight of 350-450g. Parents actually feed their chicks until they are much heavier (perhaps weighing as much as 700g), but the youngsters stay underground for a week or two after feeding has stopped, eventually being forced by hunger to leave their burrows and make their way to the sea.

Shearwater chick being weighed

Inserting your arm into a burrow can be painful if an adult is present; some can bite hard and hold on, especially if they have an egg. They are less aggressive with a chick present, probably because in the dark they can mistake the movement of a searching hand for the movements of their young. Even so, replacing chicks in a burrow with an adult must be done cautiously to avoid the parent mistakenly pecking its own offspring. The whole process is highly tactile, moving your hand from the warm, dry surface into the cool air and damp soil of the burrow. You feel cold, smooth stones, wet droppings, the brittle sticks of nesting material and then the softness of the chick, its weak bites, the touch of its tiny leathery feet. Or if

129

there is a parent in the burrow there is a harder, cooler touch of wing and adult feathers, the bulkier shape, muffled cooing calls and a sharper bite. Then, feeling underneath it, the gentler feathers of the breast and either the touch of warm down (a chick) or the curved ceramic feel of an egg yet to hatch.

Chick weighing is carried out every two days to check their growth rate and to see how feeding might alter with weather conditions and a range of other factors. Previous research suggests lower feeding rates on moonlit nights and some subsequent compensation.

After the last boat had gone, I swam in North Haven with Annette and two of her friends who were visiting for a couple of days; it seemed strange without Jess, another reminder that the first part of the Skomer season is over. The evening was clear after a hot day. Walking back to the farm after a couple of episodes of *Dexter*, a half moon hung low, a warm orange-yellow, large over the rocky tors. Looking out over the plateau from our back door, the pinprick flash of the Smalls Lighthouse pierced the dark and reminded me of an earlier conversation with Chris: Trinity House, who are the custodian of Britain's lighthouses, are selling the Skokholm light, keeper's cottage and surrounding land (romantic but inconvenient, without running water or easy access, its land peppered by densely spaced Shearwater burrows). The light itself will be replaced by a smaller super-strength LED beam, which requires much less maintenance and reflects the fact that in the age of GPS navigation the lighthouse is fast becoming obsolete. A reminder that even those comforting flashes of light, pulsing from the coast, familiar and constant, are only temporary; that these evocative signals that emphasize the distance and emptiness in this sweep of landscape may soon be gone; that the sadness of ebbing time is always with us, carrying the sweetness of the past.

And of course our lives require it, and our emotions can only be deadened by numbing stasis.

## Thoughts in Aberystwyth

It is a sunny summer's day in Aberystwyth. In the attic room in the centre of town where I write I can hear traffic on the one-way system and the sounds of builders working down the street. The sunshine streams in through the skylight from where, if I stand, I can see rooftops and chimney pots, the gardens and backyards of the Victorian townhouses on the hillside and the green canopy of Penglais woods above the town. I am relaxed, for the time being free of concerns for the future and past, happy to see friends, to see afresh the mainland, the people going about their everyday lives. Everything seems new and interesting; it is only a day after my return from Skomer for graduation week.

The feeling that I had during my first week on the island, of enjoying the 'now', is with me again. I had attributed that feeling to the peacefulness and remoteness of Skomer, but of course it is a sensation that comes with all novelty and recedes with increasing responsibility and routine: not that the island has lost its appeal or beauty, or that I do not wish to return, but that I felt a loss of that initial, uncomplicated freshness that I had expected would remain. On Skomer that freshness arises from its unique position and landscape, in Aberystwyth because I have been away so long that I can see the familiar with new eyes. It is an experience of novelty that has not yet become mundane and everyday, a flooding of senses and mind. Each new experience needs to be explored – cannot be taken for granted – and that effort of exploration suppresses pointless cycles of more introverted thought.

As patterns of life stabilise, more can be assumed. There is more space in the mind for the complexity of life to deepen; a gathering of emotional ties and shared experience that puts more at stake, bringing both rewards and difficulties. This process can lead us to a more genuine sense of fulfilment, but only if we make the effort to work through the increasing complexity to find trust and love on the other side. Without that trust in each other, the imprisoning frame of rationality and the endlessly changing world closes around us. We are forced to move on, to try again, and the only fulfilment open to us is that which comes from a constant stream of novel experience.

The Guillemots, Kittiwakes and Puffins face physical challenges that to us seem insurmountable, but they are each part of the system, safe in their role. Our minds allow us to forge our own path, to force a mistaken change and avoid our deepening role; or worse, to stand still and let chances pass us by. We can reach the heights of love that these creatures cannot, but we can also fail and slip even from the simple place in the cycle that they hold, the place we would occupy without thought.

So, stepwise logical thought can make any place, however remote and beautiful, a prison, while trust and love can make even the most unpleasant place a home. Am I saying that Skomer has become a prison to me? No! Let me try to explain: I mistook my first feelings of tranquillity, my appreciation of the landscape, the birds, nature as a whole on that unique rock, for a stable peace, an escape from change. In fact, that peacefulness was produced by the novelty of the situation; the new experiences were enough to subdue more unsettled thoughts. That type of suppression can only be sustained by a constant stream of new experience, through a chase for more that becomes consuming and must eventually end in disappointment. It is the obsessive world of the photographers who stand on Puffin burrows to get the perfect shot, shielded from discontent by the pursuit of perfection, the stream of technical complexity that occupies their thoughts, the competition to be the best. This is a lonely and distorting chase if it is allowed to go too far, a chase that has no end, that drags in time and resources to hide the emptiness of the constant change that surrounds us. This is the 'happiness' of the modern world, of individuals without community, and therefore without a stable foundation, who avoid the painful complexity needed to build such solid foundations.

The responsibilities and complexities are forced upon you in a small community: the effort required to live with others, to adapt to them, look after them, work through problems and overcome clashes. It can be frustrating; more difficult than living a separate life with only the things that you want. Individually, you can escape any unwanted interaction or viewpoint by taking refuge in technology, gaining a transient peace by engaging in constant new experience. But on the island we are forced to live together, to work around one another, to face problems and deal with them rather than walking away.

What emerges from such an effort, from those shared experiences of fitting into a group, is a simple, stable community that no longer requires the complex thought that was needed to create it, that survives through mutual trust. The problem: on the island that fulfilment lasts for only a season before each bond is broken by distance and by the rational common sense of modern life. And the only way to avoid that disintegration is to make a connection that can withstand it, that is strong enough to outweigh material concerns, that requires a step of trust to be formed. The Guillemots have bonds that hold against the forces of nature, Shearwaters retain them across thousands of miles of desolate ocean; they are part of the system, have no choice but to fit in.

Skomer, the living community of people and of nature, has helped me to put a new perspective on my feelings and experiences. The beauty of the island, its charismatic and unique fauna, its windswept isolation, is breathtaking. But in the end our fulfilment must come through building the trust that can overcome our 'rational' fears, that can allow us to enjoy life together, that gives us the confidence to take that extra step to find a connection that can last.

Main track looking south-east at dawn

19th: The weather, having first prevented me returning on Sunday, forced me to leave Aberystwyth in the grey of early morning in order to reach Martin's Haven for the nine o'clock boat. The crossing was rough, the warm dry sunshine of summer lost under glowering skies, broken seas heaving under the *Dale Princess*, salt water falling heavily over us where we sat huddled behind the cabin. And then I was back on the island for a new start, the early summer confined to memory by my stay in Aberystwyth; I could look forward once more.

After catching up with island news over a mug of tea at North Haven, I returned to the farm to unpack and to enjoy a bacon sandwich before surveying the Kittiwakes. Then I trudged down to South Stream, struck by the changes that just ten days had brought. The Wood Sage, previously low and unobtrusive with crinkled, matt-green leaves, was in flower. Its cream-coloured inflorescences carpeted every area of the plateau where Bracken was not rife, striking but still gentle in colour. The Ragwort plants are gaudy monsters in comparison: tall, solidly green, splashed yellow, clashing with the purples of the thistles and the pink of the Red Campion flowers. The brown-mottled gull chicks with their dark eyes and beaks are still dotted amongst the vegetation, but now many can fly when they choose, spreading their slender wings and gliding close to the ground, parents still nearby.

The Kittiwake chicks are also large now, with light grey, black-tipped wings, black markings interrupting the white of their heads, over-sized in the nests that previously encompassed them easily. Their size – with the exception of a few birds with small chicks – made surveying more straightforward, and by the time the day had drifted into evening I had completed the South Stream and High Cliff plots, and half of those at the Wick.

Back at the farm the volunteers were playing cricket in the yard and I joined them, my catching and batting skills – never the best – rusty from lack of practice. They invited me in for tea; roast chicken with potatoes, parsnips, onions, vegetables and gravy. Afterwards we played 'Spoons', a card game that involved trying to get four cards the same, at which point everyone had to grab for spoons laid out in the centre of the table. The number of spoons was always one less than the number of people, with the loser the person ending up without one. And it was open season in terms of how far you could go to retrieve a precious spoon from another player! A good start to the second half of the island season.

20th: This morning I completed the Kittiwake sites at the Wick and began my data input. I will need to check them again in a couple of days, when the chicks are on the verge of fledging and can be counted as 'successful'. In the afternoon Sarah was taking a group of geologists from Leicester University to look at the rock features at Tom's House. Their dissertation projects involved mapping the geology of the island, and Tom's House is an area of particular geological interest; here the basalt of the Amos outcrop meets a band of rhyolite (another volcanic rock, formed from more viscous lava than the basalt). The students showed us the flowing, folding patterns in the cliff-face, formed when the rocks were molten. On some of the boulders littering the gully these flow marks were visible as narrow banding in the rock, in delicate strips only millimetres thick.

Walking over the rocky pavement of the foreshore, we crossed 'pillows', hummocks formed when lava bubbles up and cools rapidly under water. Close to the natural arch that links Tom's House to the Basin this bubbling action is revealed again, where rounded nodules of rock protrude from the cliff-face and horizontal ledges, some little more than grape sized, others resembling half-buried basketballs. In the cliff-wall these ossified bubbles can be seen in cross-section, where molten liquid has forced through the surrounding substrate, emerging from the end of horizontal tubes of rock that resemble the undulating tubes of an intestine. Where the ends of these features had sheared away 'eyes' of quartz were visible, shot through the centre of the tubes like patterns in sticks of candy rock. The tubes stretched over the finely lined, smooth rock face; in its sandy, pinkish appearance this backdrop and the patterns it complimented reminded me of photographs of Jupiter, with its bands and the huge storm that forms its famous spot.

As the geologists sketched and took notes, Sarah and I explored the rocky shore. There were low slanting overhangs under the arm of the Amos, where the basalt was peppered with the red of oxidised iron, contorted, bulbous formations, and bands of black and grey and pinkish rock. In a rock pool at the foot of the Amos cliffs I found a Sea Slug, soft and dark amongst the green and purple seaweeds. When gently prodded with a hesitant finger, fluorescent pink areas were revealed, stunningly vivid and presumably a defensive signal. The crystal clear pools held other treasures; flesh-coloured anemones like blobs of Turkish Delight stuck to the boulders, pale pink coral coating the rocks, tendrils of fresh green weed, scuttling shrimps. Tiny fragments of the ocean world, captured for a while as in a zoo, on display in smooth crevices of black basalt, awaiting discovery, awaiting the return of the sea.

Back at the farm, James and his girlfriend Bethan made us all a meal of pasta with tuna and tomato sauce, and another day came to its end.

21$^{st}$: The majority of the day was spent working on Guillemot statistics and entering Kittiwake data onto my laptop. In the afternoon I joined Ben, who was venturing down to the sea shore at South Haven to examine a dead Seal. From Driftwood

Bay, South Haven was a beautiful sight, shimmering in the sunshine, rocks emerging from a thick carpet of Bladder Wrack, Fulmars circling and the rough grey cliffs rising on three sides to the open greenery of Skomer and the Neck. The Seal itself was not a pleasant sight, and in its decomposition emitted a powerful odour. From the size and the rounded, worn teeth we guessed it must have been fairly old when it died. It was an odd contrast to be surrounded by the beauty of the island, but to be focussed on death, decay and putrefaction where so recently there had been complexity and the subtle structure of life.

In the evening, Sarah and I joined Sue for a curry and a few games of cards before I turned in relatively early, with my last full round of Kittiwake observations planned for tomorrow.

22nd: By nine o'clock the sun was already high, and at South Stream it was hot, any dampness from the recent rain quickly evaporating from the crumbly soil, despite the tall shading Bracken. Without the Guillemots the cliffs look bare, but the Kittiwake chicks are still present, the vast majority large enough for me to count as fledged. By lunchtime I had completed South Stream, High Cliff and half of the Wick plots. The ageing summer is emphasized, at the Wick particularly, in the snow flurries of thistle seed on their cottony shuttlecocks, the well-developed 'Lesser' chicks stalking over the Puffin burrows, and in the absence of the Puffins themselves, now mostly at sea, preparing to break once more their tenuous bond with the land and head for the open oceans.

In the afternoon Sarah helped me complete the Wick sites, and we got through them relatively quickly, the Wick calm and warm, the ground on which we sat dry, radiating heat, the sea glittering; a gentle end to my surveying (excepting some final checks for small chicks, and a round of Fulmar plots in August).

The evening was spent playing cricket with the volunteers, after a can of beer with Sarah and Chris, sitting out in the evening sunshine behind our flat.

23$^{rd}$: With the main part of my survey work completed, I am able to help out with more general island work and get a more rounded experience of the daily routine that I have seen relatively little of while busy monitoring the Guillemots. This morning Chris needed help on the morning boats; the *Dale Princess* brings day trippers to the island in groups of fifty, between ten in the morning and half twelve. The visitors are met at the landing steps and shepherded to the sales point. Here they are given an introductory talk about the island: what can be seen and where, various items of housekeeping, such as the timing of return boats and the location of the visitor centre, toilets and so forth. Afterwards there is work to do answering questions, selling leaflets, postcards, bottled water and souvenirs, and hiring out binoculars. With a boat arriving every 40 minutes, the work is fairly constant, and the few quiet periods are welcome in the heat of North Haven, sheltered from the wind and under the hard gaze of the morning sun. It was good to have the chance to talk properly to the visitors and to send them off for the day with enough information to help them get the most out of their visit.

A wide range of people come over to Skomer, from the experienced birdwatchers eager to spot the rarer species to young families keen to see the Puffins and grateful even for my somewhat potted knowledge of the birds, and others uncertain what to expect from visiting the island. Their excitement at sights I see every day renewed my appreciation of the island and its importance in allowing people to experience and understand more about the natural world. By the time the last group had headed away up the track I was ready for the sandwiches I had brought for lunch. The remainder of the day passed quietly. I had agreed to help Ben and Annette with their Shearwater research overnight, and I conserved my energy before heading down to North Haven at eleven, with the last afterglow of the sunset already fading to deep blue, and the Manxies beginning to call.

Two experiments are being carried out with the Shearwaters at present. The first involves the daily weighing of chicks, and of adults arriving at and leaving their burrows. The adults are fitted with GPS devices to collect information about where they go to feed when they leave the island for the open sea. The second experiment involves the supplementary feeding of chicks in order to see if the foraging behaviour of parents is responsive to changes in the condition of their chick. The chicks are fed a mash of sardines in sunflower oil (brine can dehydrate the young birds). Birds to be fitted with GPS devices are taken from their burrow and placed in a cloth bag – the trackers are fitted back in the research lab. The chicks are weighed, and the time, chick weight and ring number of the adult is recorded, as well as the burrow they came from.

The experimental burrows are by the track that climbs the hill behind the warden's house, and through the course of a night you come to know every step of the slope. As you walk to and from the various sites, the Shearwaters fill the air, swishing overhead, fluttering in the undergrowth or, with little warning except a brief rustle of feathers, flying straight into you. I was hit by one in the face, luckily my glasses protected my eyes, and I was unscathed apart from being a little startled and feeling as if I had been hit by a weighted feather duster!

Shearwater

Once back in the research lab the adult Shearwater is held still on a foam cushion, while the tracker is taped carefully to the feathers of its back, in between the wings. Each will be recovered when the adult is next captured. Even if by some chance that does not happen, the glue holding the devices in place dissolves naturally in a matter of days. The success rate in retrieving trackers that have been deployed is 95% (in the remaining 5% of cases the tracker falls off before the bird can be recaptured), which is lucky as each costs around £40.

This evening the work rate was relaxed; tracking is being carried out simultaneously on three islands (Skomer, Copeland and Rum), and as work on Rum was not starting until the following night, Ben and Annette have to wait to begin that part of the task. Our forays into the mild night air were interspersed with cups of tea and perusal of an out-of-date copy of *The Independent*. Ben is originally from Stockport, not too far from my hometown of Macclesfield, and we have a similar (and somewhat dark) sense of humour, which I am sure is related to that area of the country. Researchers and conservationists can be very different in their interests and outlook – the latter more grounded and practical, while the pursuits of the former make for more abstract conversations that can range widely and eclectically. The mix of people on Skomer is, I think, one of the things that make the island community special, particularly for someone like me who has worked in both fields. Having people with such different perspectives working together is often valuable when deciding the best ways to look after complex ecosystems – a task that requires a whole range of skills. All in all it was an enjoyable night, with the promise of a lie-in tomorrow!

Ben and Annette at North Haven

24th: It was misty and wet when I awoke, and I spent the late morning at the computer looking at Guillemot data. After lunch I had time to go out with my Wildflower Key to do some botanising. I didn't find any rarities but was able to confirm and look in detail at some more common species I hadn't examined in a while; the mottled stem and ridged fruits of Hemlock, Rock Sea-spurrey confirmed by its wingless seeds and glandular hairs (I had suspected some larger specimens to be Greater Sea-spurrey), Lesser Burdock distinguished from Greater Burdock by its hollow basal leaves, the tiny, backward pointing prickles on the leaf edges of Marsh Bedstraw scrambling over the reeds in North Valley, and a stand of yellow-flowered Common Fleabane by East Bog. In addition, I confirmed that the bees foraging on the thistles near the farm were the Common Carder-bee, *B. pascuorum*, rather than the rarer *B. humilis* or *B. muscorum* that lack the black abdominal hairs of the more common species. It was a satisfying exploration, the first time for a long while I had been out to properly identify species at my own leisure without the pressure of the Ph.D.

In the evening, Mike and Emily (who had come over to clean the chimney at North Haven) joined Sarah, Chris and me on a fishing expedition in the island's RIB (Rigid Inflatable Boat). The sea was calm, grey-silver in the hazy evening light, rising and falling in long, slow, gentle swells as we raced across its surface, the RIB feeling almost weightless beneath us. Sarah cut the engine just off the coast at Martin's Haven, and a calm silence descended as we bobbed close to the rocks to search for Mackerel. Sarah and Mike had rods equipped with mackerel feathers as lures, lines weighted so they would pull taught beneath the surface. Compass Jellyfish, translucent, trailing their mass of thread-like appendages, drifted by, reels span as the lines were played out, and the rods were flexed back and forth to move the lures beneath the waves. After a few minutes there was sudden activity; first Sarah's rod, then Mike's bent with the pull of a fish, and out they came, flipping and glinting in the sun, their iridescent, darkly striped sides shining with delicate colour, two on one line, three on the other. They were dispatched quickly with a short wooden 'priest'.

With our fishing complete, we buzzed back towards Skomer. Suddenly out of nowhere, the grey, sickle shaped fins of Common Dolphins broke the surface ahead of us, to the left, to the right; as we approached, the huge, smooth bodies of the mammals sped beside us under the clear water, then slid upwards, breaking through the invisible skin of the waves, calves leaping clear out of the sea and splashing cleanly back down, only to leap again. A beautiful experience, shared by the *Sea Safari*, the fast sight-seeing RIB that tours the islands and turned slowly close by to enjoy the scene.

As the Common Dolphins raced west, out towards the open sea, we headed back into North Haven. A stop off Rye Rocks yielded just a single Pollock as the mist gently softened the craggy outline of the island, and Sarah and I dropped the others off at the landing steps before mooring the boat at its buoy and rowing back to the gravel beach. There was some amusement for Sarah as I took my time to work out the mechanics of paddling with a single oar, spinning us around and into the RIB a few times before I eventually found the knack and glided us up on to the beach. After Bird Log we ate the fish we had caught, seasoned with stock and paprika and fried in butter with rice. A tasty meal to finish the day, and I vowed I would order a rod of my own in time for our next trip.

25<sup>th</sup>: This morning I took the volunteers out Bracken clearing at Shearing Hays. It was good to get some practical work done, to explain the task, go through the Health and Safety talk and decide how best to tackle the job. I had forgotten how much I enjoyed the satisfaction of motivating people, telling them a bit about the work they would be doing and making a practical difference to the environment. Somehow I do not feel completely part of a place until I have worked on the land, a reflection perhaps of Lockley's own sense of the link between nature and man, expressed in his book *The Golden Year* that I had borrowed from the library at North Haven. It tells the story of a year on his Pembrokeshire farm; I hope my account of a season on Skomer is half as successful in getting across a flavour of life on this westerly outcrop of Wales.

We cleared the Bracken from a good section of the field, pulling it out at the root to prevent re-growth. At this time of year the nutrients from the plant are returning to the rhizomes below ground, and cutting has little effect on the following year's growth. Pulling the Bracken up physically therefore helps control the spread of this invasive species; its toxicity prevents the Rabbits from grazing it, and it thrives and spreads as other species are eaten around it.

Bracken does have an important role in the ecology of the island, providing food and shelter for the Skomer Vole and protection from predators for other small mammals and birds. But under heavy grazing it begins to dominate, its cover becomes dense, and other plant species cannot survive. Normally a landowner can control the plant with extensive grazing by cattle or horses; these heavy animals crush the Bracken as they move around, whilst lighter animals such as Rabbits and sheep just avoid it and its spread continues. On Skomer, with its countless Shearwater and Puffin burrows, this management is obviously not an option, and for the same reason any mechanical removal is prevented.

Our stint completed, we returned to the farm. I was ready for lunch, but in the end I only had time to grab an apple and some chocolate; there were spaces on a *Dale Princess* excursion to Grassholm, and Sue, Sarah, James and I rushed down to the landing steps to catch the boat. It always gives me a sense of adventure to head out to the open sea, the endless sweep of empty grey ocean stretching away, full of ripples and white-tipped crests that survive for a second before dissolving into that open space, explored by the Puffins that bob and dive at its surface. Fulfilling their name, Shearwaters elegantly sliced the water with their graceful wing tips as they flew low over the waves, at home in a world we can only know from the shell of a boat, heavily ploughing a narrow furrow, apart from the lives and experiences of these oceanic birds.

After perhaps an hour we reached Grassholm, and Malcolm, one of the boatmen, gave us an informal talk. Perhaps 38,000 pairs of Gannets nest on the tiny rocky outcrop, named by the Vikings when it was capped with turf. Local farmers used to bring their sheep out to enjoy the rich grass; given the distance to the island, the grazing must have been excellent to justify the trip. It is believed that, between the grazing sheep and the burrowing activities of Puffins, the soil gradually eroded away. By the 1880s, with the island a bare rock, the first Gannets arrived to start a colony that now rivals Bass Rock in size.

Gannet

The northern part of Grassholm shines white from Skomer; close up that colour dissolves into beige, guano-coated rock and the brilliant white of the Gannets, dotted in their thousands in neatly defined territories, like white shells set by an artist in concrete. Many of their chicks were large, with dark wings, close to fledging. Others were still downy white, sitting upright and gazing about them, with fluffy feathers that gave them the appearance of Suffolk sheep. The young take 90 days to fledge, and juvenile birds retain a mottled, Dalmatian-style plumage for three or four years before gaining the dazzling white, black-tipped wings and cream head of the adult birds. All have striking, clear blue eyes, contrasting with the smooth grey of their powerful beaks with which they spear fish after plummeting vertically into the ocean like darts, their two-metre wingspan folded to their sides. These are giant, graceful, Pterodactyl-like birds, a privilege to see in their isolated colony, with just the lazily bobbing Seals, a handful of Kittiwakes, Guillemots, Razorbills and Shags for company, and only the tower of the Smalls Lighthouse to punctuate the sea beyond them. We headed for home, lulled almost to sleep by the gently rolling boat, the sea air and the throbbing engine.

Back on the island, Sue and Sarah made a stir-fry, and we were joined by Helen and Ron, two of Sarah's friends, to enjoy our meal in the picnic shelter with a can of Pedigree beer to complement it. Still the day held a further adventure; James, Sarah and I walked down to the North Pond research hide to try to spot a wader seen earlier by volunteers. From the hide the wide sweep of sky over North Valley was tinged with peach as the sun drifted down to the west, and the cracked muddy plain that surrounded the remnants of the pond was crowded with 'Lessers' and their glum-looking chicks.

One chick was apparently stranded in the mud, unmoving. My initial thought was that it was best to let it be, but Sarah was adamant that we should move it. She clambered out in front of the hide but could get no further, while the chick itself flapped its muddy wings ineffectually and cheeped pitifully. Between Sarah's sad look and the forlorn struggling of the bird I softened, grimly removed my shoes and socks, and headed out onto the mud. Beyond the dry edge of the pond this was deeper than I anticipated; black, cloying, stagnant. Half way to the bird I was shin-deep, but I could still feel the firm ground beneath. Two steps away I was up to my knees, grabbing the prone chick and wading, mud covered, back to the shore, with the ungrateful bird pecking at my hand. But the mud, and the thistles I encountered on my barefoot journey back to the farm, were worth it; freed from the slime, the chick appeared uninjured and ran strongly away from us to the safety of the Bracken, calling loudly. Back at the farm I showered and washed my muddy clothes before relaxing for the rest of the evening with the volunteers, sitting out in the courtyard as the warm night deepened around us.

26th: Most of the day was spent analysing Guillemot data and starting to put together my end-of-season report on the survey methods and results. At about three I had a wander round the island with James. Despite the sun, the breeze was fresh enough for walking to be enjoyable. At Skomer Head we saw a porpoise and its calf sliding through the sun-starred waves, the afternoon ferry making its familiar way between the island and Grassholm, and two Peacock butterflies fluttering over the rocks of the headland. We continued around towards the Wick; James seems keen to take in information on the plants, insects and birds, and is quick to learn.

Answering questions is a great way of finding the limits of your knowledge. I found myself dusting off half-remembered ecological basics that I had learnt well enough and then almost forgotten as more complex knowledge built up. It was a good exercise for me to rehearse these fundamentals and to identify the areas I needed to work on. We had a pleasant stroll, seeing Gannets close to the Mew Stone (somewhat unusually – these giant, graceful birds normally frequent the north side of the island, where the fish are found in the turbulent tidal races). There were Ravens and Shags on the stone itself and a pair of Choughs foraging close to us on the sloping cliff-top. The rest of the evening passed quietly, I wrote and watched TV in the lounge, enjoying a couple of hours of solitude and contemplating the experiences of the past few days.

27th: The heat of the day made it difficult to be inside doing paperwork, and by the afternoon I was glad to be able to check the final Kittiwake nests where there had been small chicks on my last visit. The Wick seemed strangely quiet, now that the Puffins had deserted the cliff-tops. Their usual loafing spots were empty, as were the ledges and scree slopes of the Guillemot colonies I had watched for so long. By four I was finished, and Sarah, the volunteers and myself headed down to North Haven for a swim, joined later by Sue, Ben and James. The water was fairly warm now, and on diving in I felt little of the shock of the cold that made swimming a challenge during April and May. I swam to the two closest visitor buoys and back; apart from the owners of a speedboat moored in the Haven, we were alone in the water, without Puffins or Seals in attendance. Kenny had caught us Mackerel (somewhat disappointingly for Sarah, who had been looking forward to trying out her fishing rod from the landing point), and back at the farm we cooked them on a BBQ in the old farmhouse, accompanied by rice, a tomato sauce and salad.

28th - 2nd:  The last few days have drifted by without much incident; now that my survey work is all but done, my working hours are spent mainly confined to the library at North Haven, working on the Guillemot reports. Much of the island is shawled in the brash yellow of the Ragwort flowers, while the Red Campions' have shrivelled and faded, leaving worn stems and dry brown seed heads. The thistles are mainly over, white cotton replacing purple flowers, swirling up in a snowstorm under the hot sun when disturbed by passing gull chicks. The Bracken is starting to brown, and, although the Swallows still flit around the farm, the summer is definitely ageing.

Down at South Stream late one afternoon I felt the first signs of approaching autumn in the lengthened shadows, the golden light, the stillness. Of course, it is still summer, but for over a month the days have been shortening, and my perspective is altered by the end of the seabird breeding season. That expectation of autumn is a feeling that always fills me with excitement: a coming change, a new chance. I also feel a purposefulness, I guess a stirring race-memory of harvests that must be brought home, of food to collect and store, of preparations to be made for the shared challenge of winter; a communal effort that modernity has robbed us of, cleansed of the need to work to survive, of risk, of challenge, and therefore cleansed of the need to work together, separated by all we have from a simple understanding and care for each other.

Every day brings new sightings of Common Dolphins in St Bride's Bay and out towards Grassholm; pods of hundreds are either passing through or hunting. Porpoises too have been a common sight, modestly cutting through the waves with smooth triangular fins low on the water, sliding quickly under when the Dolphins boisterously burst from the sea, the young often jumping clear for an arcing, powerful second. I had been out for two more night shifts with Ben and Annette, helping with the Shearwater experiments. The chicks were large now, some over 600g and much heavier than their parents: round, heavy lumps of down with lengthening wings. Along these wings adult feathers were emerging, lined up within their waxy sheaths, making them seem plastic and artificial. Many of them cheeped loudly as they were pulled from the burrow, sometimes with difficulty given their size. Used to the supplementary feeding, they come to expect food each time they are handled. The weight these experimental chicks have gained does not push them beyond the normal range for Shearwaters, and a period of weight loss naturally precedes their emergence from the burrow to fledge.

On Tuesday, Sarah and I took a day trip to Haverfordwest. On the mainland the vegetation heralded the slide towards the end of summer, just as it had once announced its coming long before the flowers were in bloom on the windswept island. Ripened apples hung from the branches of a gnarled apple tree over the wall from The Georges' beer garden, and the green-spiked coats of conkers were large and heavy on the Horse-chestnut trees by the churchyard on the way into town. Potatoes were being harvested out on Marloes peninsular, and hay bales stood out on pale yellow fields of newly chopped grass. As always, the food at The Georges was excellent; I had Stilton and leek macaroni cheese, Sarah an impressive-looking roast duck salad, and I followed the pasta with a sweet, moist lemon and ginger pollenta cake.

Back on the island that afternoon I had a try at kayaking; James and Sarah were out in North Haven, and I wandered down to take a turn. The waters of the haven were sparkling in the afternoon sunshine, clear under the thin hull of the boat. I proceeded gingerly, trying to keep head-on to the gentle swell and improve my novice oarsman-ship. The currents in the bay are stronger than one might think gazing out from the shingle beach by the boathouse. According to Tim they continue around the edge of the haven and back out to sea, and as a result even this sheltered spot can be unpredictable. In places the light plastic kayaks surge ahead easily with the current, at other times it is an effort to turn against the flow. Despite these hazards, I enjoyed the experience, gliding out over the bay with the sun still warm where it shone down over the back of the island.

# August

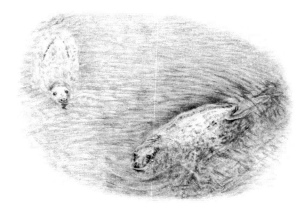

Grey Seals

3rd - 6th: Over the last couple of days I have completed the Fulmar and 'Greater' surveys, finally rounding off my fieldwork for the season and leaving the coming week to write up my end of season reports. It was hot and sunny as I toured the Fulmar sites on Friday. At Tom's House there were no large chicks at all, but there were only a handful of sites on the fissured basalt face to begin with. Round the Basin the birds have fared better, with several sites filled by soft grey, wide chicks, apparently more solid than those of the Shearwaters, with small heads and scrawny necks protruding from their downy bodies. In the heat many sat open-beaked, sometimes moving their heads back to hack out their squawking call, some alone, others with an adult sitting a foot or two away, unmoving in the midday sun.

Apart from the Fulmars and a few wheeling Kittiwakes, the Basin and the Amos were deserted, somehow belonging to that earlier part of the season, when Puffins and Razorbills lined the rocks on clear, windy days, when thousands of Guillemots crammed onto the broken rocks, and Jess watched over them from her plywood hide. Now the turquoise sea breaks onto empty rock, and the sun shines on a still landscape.

On the Neck I paused at Matthew's Wick for an afternoon nap on the warm, dry earth of the cliff-top, enjoying the peace of isolation. At Castle Bay a Seal was 'bottling': bobbing vertically in the water, nose upwards, like me enjoying the summer afternoon. As the day wore on, I joined the others for a swim and, despite the evening chill, enjoyed it, diving deep into the cold waters, bursting back up into choppy waves, cool air and fading sunshine.

On Saturday my final surveying task of the season was a trek around the 25 'Greater' nests that I had sampled earlier for breeding productivity. My purpose was to record the diet of these opportunistic predators by examining the carcasses strewn around each nest. The Shearwater wings and whole Rabbit carcasses were easy enough to identify, old bones and pellets much harder. The more I saw, however, the more I could categorise: heavier, wider Rabbit bones with strands of fur attached around the joints, the finer, lighter bones of birds, downy feathers or tiny fish vertebrae within a pellet. My finds were varied. At one nest I found crab claws and even the remains of a prawn, at another the beak of an adult Puffin and in two other nests the coloured rings of Guillemot chicks from the Amos. Manxies appear to form the bulk of the 'Greater' diet, although their bodies are also most obvious and slow to break down, so that my sample could have been biased. Rabbits made up just less than 20% of the remains, with fish, crustaceans and other birds each turning up in small numbers.

It was an interesting, but macabre day, identifying decaying bodies, chicks and adults that had lost out in the remorseless struggle for survival. At one nest I found the bodies of two large 'Greater' chicks; even these fierce birds succumb at times – the gulls are in decline, and their breeding success is only around 30% this year.

I enjoyed spending a whole day roaming the island, eating my sandwiches in the lee of Marble Rocks under a hot sun, watching rain clouds slide in over Grassholm, walking through head-high Bracken in the downpour and striding out along North Wick Ridge as the sun broke through again, glad of a fresh breeze to dispel the humid warmth the rain had brought. As the shadows lengthened, I walked over Captain Kites to North Haven, my survey work for the season completed.

Dinner included fresh mackerel, caught by Kenny and served with a Thai-style sauce and rice. Another week on the island drew to a close with a sociable, wine-softened evening. Tim Healing (who has returned to the island for a second bout of Skomer Vole surveying) joined us for the meal. He is a large, jovial fellow, but his genial manner belies a sharp mind; he has a wealth of experience in many fields, from mammalian and epidemiological research, to working with the UN on disaster relief. He has been visiting the island for many years and led the Skomer Vole survey that I helped with on my first stay on Skomer. I remembered his love of conversation, and of red wine; he is an entertaining storyteller when he gets going.

He told us about life on the island twenty or thirty years ago, when RAF Brawdy was still operational, and night-time exercises often took place over the islands. When these manoeuvres required aircraft to fly fully laden with ballast, the offices would call Skomer and ask if any materials were needed on the island. If so these would form the ballast, being dropped off on the island after the exercise was complete. One year the warden and his wife were stranded over Christmas, and the RAF dropped them a Christmas meal and a tree.

There were other practical implications resulting from the close proximity of military installations to the island. During the Cold War, a sonar system for tracking Russian submarines extended from Brawdy out into the Atlantic, and as a result tankers bound for Milford Haven could only anchor in the southern half of St Bride's Bay to avoid damage to the underwater cables. Many of Tim's stories emphasized the communal spirit that extended well beyond Skomer, taking in the local community as well as the military in a very human, informal and trusting network of people. They were happy to help one another and, in doing so, shared experiences and created many stories; these are things that would never have happened had they kept themselves to themselves and looked out only for their own interests.

The inventive ways that people shared their skills, making small adjustments to their own work to help others, demonstrated to me the best of human creativity. Systems worked because they integrated the needs of different people; they were not just driven by a desire to make profit – but were solid and beneficial to all. Groceries were supplied to the island from a store owned by one of the wardens and his wife, so that visitors had a much lighter load to carry to the island, and the profits from the same store were used to buy many of the books in the library at North Haven. For several years the son of one warden was ferried to school and home in the evening by an extra boat, the fee paid for by the local council, the service being very useful to anyone on the island who fancied a whole day on the mainland without worrying about the time of the last ferry.

Well Field and the farm

Back then, most of the accommodation on Skomer was in the old research base at North Haven; this close proximity of people and the basic facilities (gas lamps in rooms, a single water tank that made washing a rare treat) brought a comradeship that is hard to match with our well-appointed but separate living spaces. Given the choice, personal space is of course preferred by most – me included, but being forced to co-exist carries many rewards that make it worth the effort. I get the feeling that Tim misses those more sociable days, and I think I agree with him; something is lost as facilities improve and people move out into their own spaces. But even with the new facilities, island life brings a rare sense of community, often lost in the sprawling estates of modern towns and cities.

7th - 8th: On Monday Sarah was away, and I was able to spend some time with the volunteers, setting them to work carrying out vegetation surveys within the Rabbit exclosures. In many places the differences in vegetation within and outside the exclosures is striking. Within the fencing, where they are in competition with grasses and Heather, Bracken and Ragwort hardly occur; this is particularly noticeable in South Park. Here a dense yellow blanket of Ragwort flowers is interrupted by the fenced square, which is brown with long grasses, flecked with the white of Yarrow and the purple of opening heather flowers.

Rabbits were introduced to Skomer in medieval times, when the island was managed as a warren, with fur and meat sold to the mainland. Over hundreds of years many different varieties have been brought on to augment stocks, and as a result the population displays a range of colours, from the familiar grey-brown to black, white and piebald. The Rabbits are not farmed commercially nowadays, but they certainly have a big impact on the ecology of the island. In some ways their influence is positive; grazing prevents vigorous plants out-competing other species, while old burrows are often taken over by Puffins and Shearwaters. But there is a down side; plants such as Bracken and Ragwort are toxic and avoided by the Rabbits, and these plants can spread and dominate as more edible species are overgrazed. Excessive burrowing also leaves the ground ever more fragile, while Puffins and Shearwaters are well adapted to dig their own burrows if they need to.

There is an ongoing debate on the merits of controlling the Rabbit population, with differences of opinion on the possible effect on the bird colonies of reducing the numbers of these familiar mammals. This is just one of the dilemmas that face those charged with looking after special places such as Skomer, where systems are not just collections of individual species living independently but complex webs of interaction. These issues make vegetation monitoring important, although at times our efforts are thwarted when Rabbits break into the exclosures to enjoy the lush vegetation within. The volunteers were keen to get involved in the survey work and, over the day, completed the majority of the sites with little input from me, aside from the identification of a few plant species and some advice on the placement of quadrats.

In the afternoon I was able to read up some of the history of the island in Howell's book *The Sounds Between*. From this I learnt that the lime kilns that overlook North Haven date from the 18th and 19th centuries and were used to produce lime to fertilize crops and sweeten grass, and as a component of the mortar used in the island buildings. Limestone and coal were landed by barge in the haven and transported by horse and cart to the kilns. I also learnt that Abysinnia (an old field between the farm and Skomer Head) was probably named in the 19th century around the time of the war of 1867-68 between Britain and Theodore of Abysinnia, fought in Ethiopia.

These tit-bits of information, along with a look at some books on Seals and Cetaceans, were to stand me in good stead on Tuesday. With the seas fairly rough, Sue left on the nine o'clock boat to take her friend to the station and, with Sarah and Chris away, I took over the supervision of the morning boats and the routine of the introductory talks. It was good to have the chance to chat to the visitors and pass on some of the things I had learnt, and the sunny morning was further improved by the delivery by Kenny of my first fishing rod and reel, which he managed to get hold of for only £20. Now I needed to catch some fish!

9th - 12th:  On Wednesday morning I was on boats again; there were fewer people and my practice with the talks the previous day helped me to vary what I said a little. After the ten o'clock boat I expected to have time to spend an hour or so clearing Bracken with the volunteers, but we had only just started when Kenny called to say he was putting on another two trips. Sarah – one of the volunteers – and I hurried down to North Haven just as the visitors were reaching the top of the steps, and I was able to give a slightly breathless introduction to the island. Between boats we sheltered in the old lime kiln; although it was a sunny day, a breeze was blowing dust from the burrows down the track and into our faces where we sat at the sales-point. It was a tiny example of how burrowing and dry weather can quickly cause erosion, blowing the precious layer of soil out into the sea.

After lunch I worked with the volunteers clearing more Bracken, which James collected in the tractor to be stored in the outbuilding in the corner of the farm garden. We filled the small hut to the roof, hopefully providing a good supply for the compost loos. Once dried the dead material soaks up the effluent, helping it to decompose and break down into compost, while at the same time suppressing odours. With 250 people per day using the facilities in high season, getting the composting process right is essential and an ongoing task.

In the evening we enjoyed a meal of sausages and burgers, Sue's delicious potato wedges, a stir-fry of vegetables and bacon, and some salad as a nod to healthy eating. Afterwards, with the night dark under thickening cloud, I walked to North Haven to help Ben and Annette, now on the final nights of the

Shearwater tracking experiments. They had only four GPS birds left to retrieve and were hopeful this would be their last night of work; both were pretty tired, and my presence was as much a matter of moral support as of practical help.

The birds were slow to return, although it was an overcast night, with sharp bursts of rain blowing off the sea as we worked. Above the cloud, unseen, was a full moon, and it has been suggested that the Shearwaters alter their visits according to the timing of the moon's cycle, even if specific weather conditions would offer them a safe night to land. Whatever the reason, we did not retrieve any GPS birds and turned in at around half past four after a sociable but fruitless night.

North Castle early morning

Thursday passed quietly (I only woke up at lunchtime!), but I managed to get in a swim, making it out across the bay to the third visitor buoy, unknown to me followed by an inquisitive Seal for part of the distance. It felt liberating to cross so much of the bay under the prow of a moored yacht and into the waters beneath the cliffs of the Neck, where the Seals bob and pull themselves up onto Rye Rocks to bask.

On Friday I left the island for a weekend in Aberystwyth, using the opportunity to take back some of my kit. When I return on Tuesday I will only have four more days on Skomer before my stay is over.

16th - 18th: My last week on Skomer went by fast. On Tuesday I travelled back from Aberystwyth in a somewhat reflective mood. Already the months I have spent away have distanced me from the town, from a view of it as home. My friends are planning for the future, thinking of leaving, and I still felt a little unsettled by the change as we crossed Jack Sound, and Skomer loomed ahead. Soon I will be moving on from this home as well.

Wednesday and Thursday passed in a round of report writing, emails and cups of tea at North Haven. Holly is back from Rum, and it was good to catch up, relax and let time drift by. On Thursday afternoon I helped her with the Manxie chick weighing; although the tracking experiments have finished, the chicks will be weighed each day until fledging to chart their development. Many are losing their down, with patches of smooth black and white adult feathers interspersed with thick grey fluff. The results can be comical; one chick had adult plumage around its face with the down behind resembling a huge 'Afro' haircut, another had a strip of down along the top of its head like a Mohican. The chicks that are closer to fledging are starting to lose some of the weight that sustained them in the burrow, the heaviest around 550g rather than over 700g. But they are much more solid and compact, building the robust structure that will help them withstand the fury of the Atlantic weather on their long migration south.

On Thursday morning I took a walk round the island and wrote a short description:

> 'Stepping out into the courtyard this morning, the softness of the air has a new edge, a coolness that is not yet a chill but betrays the changing season. For the first time the shifting colours of the island mark senescence rather than the appearance of new flowers. Crisp brown is gently spreading from leaf tips of Bracken and Bramble, darkening the yellow blooms of the Ragwort. Along the path through North Valley the volunteers have been scything back the vegetation, and the scatter of cut Bracken over the path is like a harvest.

> At the stream the Water Dropwort stems are brittle and dead, the carpet of Creeping Forget-me-not reduced to a few pale-flowered plants under the Willow leaves, themselves tarnished and fading. In the Rabbit exclosures the purple haze of Heather flowers alone defies the coming autumn, and bees twist and turn between the inflorescences. The air is still, and there is a quietness; the island is peaceful after the frantic race to breed and fledge young, to protect new life.

> Here on the north coast a gentle breeze ruffles the pages of my notepad, the lobster-pot men work below me off the Garland Stone and the sounds of the boat's engine and various clatters and mechanical noises drift up to me. From half a mile away the hum of generators on the stationary tankers percolates the

*silence. Although it is eleven in the morning, the light has the
quality of a late afternoon; the warmth of the sun is lessened
by high cloud, and in the clear air the fissures and colours of
the rocks are picked out precisely. There is an air of waiting.
Even the sea is tranquil, though in the tidal race the
smoothness is an illusion that hides turmoil beneath.*

*Waves lap at the foot of the Garland Stone – hard now to
imagine those spring storms, when spray crested its rocky peak.
Glancing up, I can see the Irish ferry, my old friend, white
against the grey of sea and sky, drifting through the stillness.'*

Despite the autumnal feel to the island, I was still able to enjoy
an afternoon nap in the sunshine at South Stream cliffs. In fact,
it was almost too warm lying on the soft dry earth amidst the
Sea Campion and Sea Mayweed, the heat of the sun stored by
the ground and radiated back, humidly exhaled from deep
stands of Bracken, bounced from rocks. I slept without the
background chorus of bird cries that formed the soundtrack to
the early season. There were no Guillemots to utter their
throaty exclamations, no deep croaking Razorbills, and the
Kittiwakes too had left their nest spots, with the last one or two
circling off the coast, their calls a faint reprise of the orchestral
wall of sound that existed before. In the bay, kelp drifted lazily
in the placid waters, and the waves lapped the rocks with barely
a sound.

19th:  Friday arrived, my last full day on the island. Sarah and I
were on morning boats, and I gave an introductory talk for the
final time. Between the boats we played cards in the old lime
kiln. Through the afternoon the sky grew overcast, and a cool
easterly wind picked up. Still, I was determined to have a last

swim, and, alone, walked down to the landing point, observed from the warmth of the research kitchen by Sarah, Holly and Chris. I paused longer than usual where the waters ebbed and flowed over the steps; the chill wind and grey skies gave the sea a cold, unwelcoming look. Then I was in, the waves closing over me as I dived and surged back up, emerging again and starting to swim in one movement before the cold took hold.

I made the first visitor buoy and clung on, remembering those afternoons in May and June when we had crowded around the white bobbing marker to catch our breath under a warm sun, with rafts of Puffins close by and the long summer ahead of us. Then I pushed on, my short-sighted eyes focussed fuzzily on the furthest buoy, the yacht moored up in the haven slipping past as I made for the headland of the Neck. As the rocky shore drew closer, I again felt that sense of freedom that comes with even modest exploration, moving out beyond the usual extent of our swims into the lea of the other shore. The last yards seemed to stretch out in front of me, and I felt I was barely moving, until at last the waving mass of kelp reached out from the rocks, and I glided in amongst the soft fronds to rest, clutching the barnacle-covered stone. I turned to look out at North Haven from my new position, seeing clouds racing over the island, grey water all round, to the north fading across St Bride's Bay to the distant shore of St David's peninsular.

After a few seconds I began my return journey. Away from the shore, the wind furrowed the waters of the bay and spray flecked my face, so that it was almost warmer to swim a few strokes beneath the surface. I was colder now and, as the rain clouds darkened the southern sky, felt slightly anxious as well as exhilarated by my position. Soon, however, that welcoming first visitor buoy was close, and I was back within our normal bounds, and within another few minutes I dragged myself up on to the steps, tired and cold but happy to have achieved my goal and grateful to accept a cup of tea at North Haven.

Later, we gathered for my leaving night, a shared meal in Sue's kitchen; as usual a friendly and happy evening. Sarah had organised a card, with messages even from Jess and Maria. After eating, we headed down to Chris's for a few whiskies, listening to music with disco lights provided by twirling a colander on top of a flashlight. All too soon we were walking back, the familiar tanker lights gleaming over the bay, the Manxies whirring and fluttering round us in the dark, the island night surrounding us.

20th: As always, leaving is hardest in the light of the morning, when bags are packed, familiar items cleared away. I had time to stroll out to Bull Hole; the island was enclosed by low drifting clouds that softened the horizon, the purple heather on the north coast, the Garland Stone, the shapes of the moored ships. The rock-studded country was as sweeping, open and romantically desolate as when I saw it on my first day.

Back at the farm Sarah made me a cup of tea before she headed out to drive my kit down to the landing steps on the tractor. I will miss her, and the others. At the steps everyone was waiting despite the wind and rain: Dave, Annette, Holly, Sue, Chris, Sarah and James. Last photos were taken, final goodbyes said, and then I was in the boat, the landing steps drifting away as we moved off, everyone waving. As we left North Haven, I was forced for a moment to turn away from the visitors who were sharing the trip back to the mainland. Skomer receded, the shawl of mist from which she had emerged on that first April afternoon gently concealing the island again.

# References and Further Reading

(Where references are cited in the text, the page number on which they are mentioned is given in brackets. References without page numbers are suggestions for further reading)

Buxton, J. and Lockley, R.M. (1950) *Island of Skomer*. Staples Press, London

Driver, T. (2007) *Pembrokeshire: Historic Landscapes from the air*. Royal Commission on the Ancient and Historical Monuments of Wales, Aberystwyth

Ford, E.B. (1975) *Ecological Genetics, Fourth Edition*. Chapman and Hall, London [pp 27]

Howells, R. (1968) *The sounds between: The story of the islands of Skomer, Skokholm, Ramsey and Grassholm and of those who have sought to wrest a living from them*. Gomerian P., Llandysul [pp 101]

Lockley, R.M. (1974) *Seal Woman*. Rex Collings Ltd, London [pp 59]

Lockley, R.M. (1948) *The Golden Year*. Witherby, London [pp 91]

Matthews, J. (2011) *Skomer: Portrait of a Welsh Island*. Graffeg, Cardiff

Rose, F. (2006) *The Wild Flower Key: How to identify wild flowers trees and shrubs in Britain and Ireland, Revised Edition*. Frederick Warne, London [pp 90]

Watson, A.J. and Lovelock, J.E. (1983) Biological homeostasis of the global environment: The parable of Daisyworld. *Tellus B* **35**(4) 286-289 [pp 32]

Wright, S. (1932) The roles of mutation, inbreeding, crossbreeding and selection in evolution. *Proceedings of the Sixth Annual Congress of Genetics* 1: 356-366 [pp 27]

# Species List
## (species seen on the mainland listed below)

## Plants

| | |
|---|---|
| Bittersweet | *Solanum dulcamara* L. |
| Blackthorn | *Prunus spinosa* L. |
| Bluebells | *Hyacinthoides non-scriptus* (L.) Chouard *ex* Rothm. |
| Bog Pimpernel | *Anagallis tenella* L. |
| Bracken | *Pteridium aquilinum* (L.) Kuhn |
| Bramble | *Rubus fruticosus* agg. *sensu lato* |
| Common Fleabane | *Pulicaria dysenterica* (L.) Bernh. |
| Common Scurvygrass | *Cochlearia officinalis* L. |
| Common Sorrel | *Rumex acetosa* L. |
| Creeping Buttercup | *Ranunculus repens* L. |
| Creeping Forget-me-not | *Myosotis secunda* Al. Murray |
| Early Forget-me-not | *Myosotis ramosissima* Rochel |
| Elder | *Sambucus nigra* L. |
| English Stonecrop | *Sedum anglicum* Huds. |
| Common Gorse | *Ulex europaeus* L. |
| Field Forget-me-not | *Myosotis arvensis* (L.) Hill |
| Common Figwort | *Scrophularia nodosa* L. |
| Goat Willow | *Salix caprea* L. |
| Gypsywort | *Lycopus europaeus* L. |
| Heath Bedstraw | *Galium saxatile* L. |
| Hemlock Water Dropwort | *Oenanthe crocata* L. |
| Hemlock | *Conium maculatum* L. |
| Knotted Pearlwort | *Sagina nodosa* (L.) Fenzl. |
| Lesser Burdock | *Arctium minus* (Hill) Bernh. |

| | |
|---|---|
| Lesser Celandine | *Ficaria verna* Huds. |
| Lesser Spearwort | *Ranunculus flammula* L. |
| Marsh Pennywort | *Hydrocotyle vulgaris* L. |
| Marsh Bedstraw | *Galium palustre* L. |
| Nettle | *Urtica dioica* L. |
| Procumbent Pearlwort | *Sagina procumbens* L. |
| Purple Loosestrife | *Lythrum salicaria* L. |
| Ragwort | *Senecio jacobaea* L. |
| Red Campion | *Silene dioica* (L.) Clairv. |
| Rock Sea-spurrey | *Spergularia rupicola* Lebel *ex* Le Jol. |
| Scarlet Pimpernel | *Anagallis arvensis* L. |
| Sea Campion | *Silene uniflora* Roth. |
| Sea Mayweed | *Tripleurospermum maritinum* (L.) W.D.J. Koch |
| Selfheal | *Prunella vulgaris* L. |
| Silverweed | *Potentilla anserine* L. |
| Skullcap | *Scutellaria galericulata* L. |
| Square-stalked St John's-wort | *Hypericum tetrapterum* Fr. |
| Three-lobed Water-crowfoot | *Ranunculus tripartitus* DC. |
| Thrift | *Armeria maritima* subsp *maritima* (Mill.) Willd. |
| Water Mint | *Mentha aquatica* L. |
| Water Pepper | *Persicaria hydropiper* (L.) Delabre |
| Wood Sage | *Teucrium scorodonia* L. |
| Yarrow | *Achillea millefolium* L. |
| Yorkshire Fog | *Holcus lanatus* L. |

## Birds

| | |
|---|---|
| Atlantic Puffin | *Fratercula arctica* (Linnaeus, 1758) |
| Barn Owl | *Tyto alba* (Scopoli, 1769) |

| | |
|---|---|
| Blackcap | *Sylvia atricapilla* (Linnaeus, 1758) |
| Canada Goose | *Branta canadensis* (Linnaeus, 1758) |
| Chiffchaff | *Phylloscopus collybita* (Vieillot, 1817) |
| Chough | *Pyrrhocorax pyrrhocorax* (Linnaeus, 1758) |
| Common Buzzard | *Buteo buteo* (Linnaeus, 1758) |
| Curlew | *Numenius arquata* (Linnaeus, 1758) |
| Fulmar | *Fulmarus glacialis* (Linnaeus, 1761) |
| Gannet | *Sula bassana* (Linnaeus, 1758) |
| Golden Oriole | *Oriolus oriolus* (Linnaeus, 1758) |
| Grasshopper Warbler | *Locustella naevia* (Boddaert, 1783) |
| Great Black-backed Gull | *Larus marinus* Linnaeus, 1758 |
| Guillemot | *Uria aalge* (Pontopiddan, 1763) |
| Herring Gull | *Larus argentatus* Pontopiddan, 1763 |
| Jackdaw | *Corvus monedula* Linnaeus, 1758 |
| Kittiwake | *Rissa tridactyla* (Linnaeus, 1758) |
| Lesser Black-backed Gull | *Larus fuscus* Linnaeus, 1758 |
| Linnet | *Carduelis cannabina* (Linnaeus, 1758) |
| Little Owl | *Athene noctua* (Scopoli, 1769) |
| Manx Shearwater | *Puffinus puffinus* (Brünnich, 1764) |
| Meadow Pipit | *Anthus pratensis* (Linnaeus, 1758) |
| Moorhen | *Gallinula chloropus* (Linnaeus, 1758) |
| Oystercatcher | *Haematopus ostralegus* Linnaeus, 1758 |
| Raven | *Corvus corax* Linnaeus, 1758 |
| Razorbill | *Alca torda* Linnaeus, 1758 |

| | |
|---|---|
| Reed Bunting | *Emberiza schoeniclus* (Linnaeus, 1758) |
| Sedge Warbler | *Acrocephalus schoenobaenus* (Linnaeus, 1758) |
| Shag | *Phalacrocorax aristotelis* (Linnaeus, 1761) |
| Short-eared Owl | *Asio flammeus* (Pontoppidan, 1763) |
| Shoveler | *Anas clypeata* Linnaeus, 1758 |
| Storm Petrel | *Hydrobates pelagicus* (Linnaeus, 1758) |
| Whitethroat | *Sylvia communis* Latham, 1787 |
| Willow Warbler | *Phylloscopus trochilus* (Linnaeus, 1758) |

## Invertebrates

| | |
|---|---|
| Common Blue damselfly | *Enallagma cyathigerum* (Charpentier, 1840) |
| Common Carder-bee | *Bombus pascuorum* (Scopoli, 1763) |
| Glow-worm | *Lampyris noctiluca* (Linnaeus, 1758) |
| Scarab beetles | *Scarabaeoidea* Latreille, 1802 |
| Cinnabar moth | *Tyria jacobaeae* (Linnaeus, 1758) |
| Dark Green Fritillary | *Argynnis aglaja* (Linnaeus, 1758) |
| Large Skipper | *Ochlodes venata* (Esper, 1777) |
| Meadow Brown | *Maniola jurtina* (Linnaeus, 1758) |
| Peacock butterfly | *Inachis io* (Linnaeus, 1758) |
| Ringlet | *Aphantopus hyperantus* (Linnaeus, 1758) |
| Small Copper | *Lycaena phlaeas* (Linnaeus, 1761) |

## Mammals

| | |
|---|---|
| Common Shrew | *Sorex araneus* Linnaeus, 1758 |

| European Rabbit | *Oryctolagus cuniculus* (Linnaeus, 1758) |
| Skomer Vole | *Myodes glareolus* subsp. *skomerensis* |

## Marine life

| Common Dolphin | *Delphinus delphis* Linnaeus, 1758 |
| Grey Seal | *Halichoerus grypus* (Fabricius, 1791) |
| Harbour Porpoise | *Phocoena phocoena* (Linnaeus, 1758) |
| Garfish | *Belone belone* (Linnaeus, 1761) |
| Mackerel | *Scomber scombrus* Linnaeus, 1758 |
| Pollock | *Pollachius pollachius* (Linnaeus, 1758) |
| Ocean Sunfish | *Mola mola* (Linnaeus, 1758) |
| Compass Jellyfish | *Chrysaora hysoscella* (Linnaeus, 1766) |
| Sea Gooseberry | *Pleurobrachia pileus* (O. F. Müller, 1776) |
| Bladder Wrack | *Fucus vesiculosus* Linnaeus |
| Kelps | *Laminaria* spp. J.V. Lamouroux, 1813 |

## Mainland Plants (excluding cultivated species)

| Alexanders | *Smyrnium olusatrum* L. |
| Ash | *Fraxinus excelsior* L. |
| Broad-leaved Dock | *Rumex obtusifolius* L. |
| Common Mouse-ear | *Cerastium holosteoides* Baumg. |
| Common Toadflax | *Linaria vulgaris* Mill. |
| Cow Parsley | *Anthriscus sylvestris* (L.) Hoffm. |
| Enchanter's Nightshade | *Circaea lutetiana* L. |
| Foxglove | *Digitalis purpurea* L. |
| Garlic Mustard | *Alliaria petiolata* (M. Bieb.) Cavara & Grande |
| Germander Speedwell | *Veronica chaemedrys* L. |

| | |
|---|---|
| Horse-chestnut | *Aesculus hippocastanum* L. |
| Lime | *Tilia x europaea* L. |
| Red Valerian | *Centranthus ruber* (L.) DC. |
| Sheep's bit Scabious | *Jasione montana* L. |
| Sycamore | *Acer pseudoplatanus* L. |
| Wild Garlic (Ramsons) | *Allium ursinum* L. |
| Wood Avens | *Geum urbanum* L. |
| Wych Elm | *Ulmus glabra* Huds. |
| Yellow Iris | *Iris pseudacorus* L. |

## Mainland Birds

| | |
|---|---|
| Robin | *Erithacus rubecula* (Linnaeus, 1758) |

## Mainland Insects

| | |
|---|---|
| Common Blue butterfly | *Polyommatus icarus* (Rottemburg, 1775) |
| Scarlet Tiger moth | *Callimorpha dominula* (Linnaeus, 1758) |

# Acknowledgements

I would like to thank the Wildlife Trust of South and West Wales for the opportunity to work on Skomer Island, and the Joint Nature Conservation Committee for funding my post.

Skomer's volunteers, staff and researchers made my season on the island a special one. Particular thanks to Chris Taylor, the island's warden during my stay, purveyor of Old Speckled Hen and source of lots of island knowledge; assistant warden Sarah Harris, who put up with me as a house mate, drew the map of the island in this book and shared her expert bird knowledge (as well as many stories about the Calf of Man!); Sue Williams, visitor services officer, great character, friend and (vitally important) cook; Dave Boyle, another great source of island knowledge and birding expertise, and (perhaps more importantly) the only other football fan on the island in 2011!

Thanks to Jess Meade, for invaluable advice on Guillemots and their ways, lots of swimming excursions, crosswords and many laughs. To the Oxford research team: Ben Dean, Holly Kirk and Annette Fayet, who brought a lot of humour to the island, as well as letting me get involved with their work and providing a wealth of information on shearwaters. And a special mention for Annette for some great desserts (recipes at the back of the book!). Thanks also to the boatmen, especially Carl and Kenny, for sharing their knowledge, experience and Mackerel!

The weekly volunteers are essential to running the island and offer comradeship, food and occasionally dangerous evening card games! Long-term volunteers Maria Gill (animal and wildlife artist) and James Roden also added much to island life.

And, last but not least, thanks to the visiting experts who were generous with their knowledge and time and have added much colour to this journal, especially Tim Healing, Skomer Vole researcher and entertaining story teller.

# Useful Organisations and Contacts

**Wildlife Trust of South and West Wales**: Information about reserves, events and conservation work, including details on visiting Skomer as a volunteer or overnight guest.
http://www.welshwildlife.org

**Sea Trust**: The marine arm of the Wildlife Trust of South and West Wales; site includes details of how to get involved in surveys, information on boat trips and local sea sightings.
http://seatrust.org.uk/

**Skomer Island Blog**: the official island blog, for island and wildlife news.
http://skomerisland.blogspot.co.uk

**Pembrokeshire Coast National Park**: The official national park website, with lots of useful local information.
http://www.pembrokeshirecoast.org.uk

**Pembrokeshire Tourist Information**: General information on things to do and places to stay in Pembrokeshire.
http://www.visitpembrokeshire.com

**Pembrokeshire Boat Trips**: Details of sightseeing trips around Pembrokeshire, including trips to Skomer.
http://www.pembrokeshire-islands.co.uk

**Oxford University Research**: Find out more about the seabird research carried out by Oxford University scientists on the island, including a list of their publications.
http://oxnav.zoo.ox.ac.uk/seabirds

**British Trust for Ornithology**: Information and news about British birds, including how to get involved in surveying and ringing.
http://www.bto.org/

**Royal Society for the Protection of Birds**: Charity working to protect birds and their habitats; including bird ID guides and details of how to get involved with this important work.
http://www.rspb.org.uk/

**Joint Nature Conservation Committee**: Website of the organisation that provides advice to the British government on conservation.
http://jncc.defra.gov.uk/

**Sea Watch Foundation**: Information on Cetaceans and other marine life; includes details of how to get involved by reporting sightings or volunteering.
http://seawatchfoundation.org.uk/

**The Mammal Society**: Information and news about British mammals, from dolphins to voles; details of local mammal groups and how to get involved with recording.
http://www.mammal.org.uk/

**Linda Norris**: website of a local artist who has strong ties to Skomer.
http://www.linda-norris.com

**Meg Ghyll Pet and Wildlife Pencil Art**: website of one of the long-term volunteers, Maria, who produces great drawings of animals and illustrated the interpretation boards in the island's bird hides.
http://www.megghyll.co.uk

# Annette's Recipes

## Tarte au citron meringuée /
## Lemon-Meringue Tart

For 6-8 persons

- 1 shortcrust pastry (or short pastry) roll

*For the lemon cream*:

- 4 lemons
- 150g caster sugar
- 3 eggs
- 1 tbsp corn flour

*For the meringue*:

- 2 egg whites
- 100g caster sugar
- 1 tsp baking powder

Preheat oven to 180°C. Lay the pastry in a tart tin, prick with a fork and bake blind for 20-25 minutes (until cooked and golden).

*Lemon cream:*

Beat the eggs in a bowl. Wash the lemons and use a grater to collect the zest of 3 of them. Squeeze the juice from all 4 lemons. Warm the lemon juice, sugar, corn flour, and lemon zest over a low heat, stirring regularly with a whisk. Once the mixture is warm, slowly stir in the beaten eggs. Increase the heat and continue to stir until about half a minute after the mixture has thickened. Pour onto the blind-baked pastry case and leave to cool for at least 2 hours, until set.

*Meringue (better to do this just before serving):*
Preheat the oven to 120°C. Beat the egg whites with a pinch of salt until very stiff. Add the sugar and baking powder and beat for a further minute or so until the sugar has dissolved. The mix should look glossy. Spread the meringue over the lemon base. Put in the oven for about 10 minutes, or until the top of the meringue starts to turn golden.

# Triple Chocolate Tart

For 6-8 persons (depending on appetite!)

- 1 pack of cookies or digestive biscuits

- 2 teaspoons butter

- 3 x 300ml milk

- 3 x 200ml crème fraîche

- 150g white chocolate

- 150g milk chocolate

- 200g dark chocolate

- 3 tbsps of gelatine

Put the cookies in a plastic bag and crush them into crumbs using a rolling pin. Melt the butter and add to the crushed cookies until the mixture forms an even paste. Spread the paste (1-2cm thick) in a 'spring-from' tin and place in the fridge.

Put the gelatine in cold water (1/4 cup of water for each tablespoon of gelatine) and leave it for 10 minutes to swell. In a saucepan, warm 250ml of milk and 250ml of crème fraîche. Add the white chocolate to the warm milk/cream mixture. Stir with a whisk until the chocolate has melted. Warm a third of the gelatine over hot water. When it becomes liquid, add to the chocolate mixture and stir until smooth. Allow to cool for about 10 minutes, then pour over the biscuit base and leave in the fridge for at least 2 hours, until set. Repeat the steps above to make a similar mixture with the milk chocolate and the dark chocolate, adding each mixture to the previous chocolate layer once it has set.

# *Other birding books by Brambleby Books*

*Arrivals and Rivals – A duel for the winning bird*
Adrian Riley
ISBN 9780954334796

*UK500: Birding in the fast lane*
James Hanlon
ISBN 9780954334789

*Winging it – Birding for Low-flyers*
Andrew Fallan
ISBN 9780955392856

*The Ruffled Edge – Notes from a Nature Warden*
Pete Howard
ISBN 9781908241061

*Birduder 344 – A life list ordinary*
Rob Sawyer
ISBN 9781908241092

*Scilly Birding – Joining the Madding Crowd*
Simon Davey
ISBN 9781908241177

*A-Z of Birds – A birder's tale from around the world*
Bo Beolens
ISBN 9781908241238

www.bramblebybooks.co.uk